Jerusalem I
From the Bronze Age to the Maccabees

CITIES OF THE BIBLICAL WORLD

Jerusalem I

From the Bronze Age to the Maccabees

Graeme Auld
Professor of Hebrew Bible, University of Edinburgh

Margreet Steiner
*Honorary Fellow, Department of Archaeology,
University of Leiden*

THE LUTTERWORTH PRESS (L)
CAMBRIDGE

MERCER UNIVERSITY PRESS
USA

First published in the UK by:
The Lutterworth Press
P.O. Box 60
Cambridge
CB1 2NT
ISBN 0 7188 2901 8

First published in the USA by:
Mercer University Press
6316 Peake Road
Macon
Georgia 31210-39601
USA
ISBN 086554 520 0

British Library Cataloguing in Publication Data:
A catalogue record is available from the British Library.

Printed in Great Britain by
Hillman Printers (Frome) Ltd, Frome, Somerset

CITIES OF THE BIBLICAL WORLD

General Editor:
Graham I. Davies, Lecturer in Divinity, Cambridge University.

Other Titles:
Excavation in Palestine, Roger Moorey, Senior Assistant Keeper, Department of Antiquities, Ashmolean Museum, Oxford.
Jericho, John R. Bartlett, Lecturer in Divinity, and Fellow of Trinity College, Dublin.
Megiddo, Graham I. Davies.
Qumran, Philip R. Davies, Lecturer in Biblical Studies, University of Sheffield.
Ugarit (Ras Shamra), Adrian H. W. Curtis, Lecturer in Old Testament Studies, University of Manchester.

Of related interest:
A Century of Biblical Archaeology, Roger Moorey.
Archaeology of the Land of the Bible 10.000-586 B.C.E., Amihai Mazar.

Contents

Acknowledgements

All the illustrations were prepared by Eric van Driel, to whom we are much indebted.

Copyright of the other plans or plates we gratefully acknowledge as follows: Figure 2, Israel Exploration Society; Figures 4 and 22, Palestine Exploration Fund; Figures 7 and 33, British School of Archaeology in Jerusalem; Figure 11, Staatlich Museen, Berlin; Figure 19, Schweizerisches Katholisches Bibelwerk; Figure 38, Israel Museum; Figure 39, Hamish Auld.

List of Illustrations

Preface

It is daunting to add yet another volume to the many already published on Jerusalem. We have, however, appreciated the invitation and encouragement of editor and publishers to prepare this short book. The idea of writing it together was appropriately born in Jerusalem, when both authors were resident in the British School of Archaeology in June 1990 during the Second International Congress on Biblical Archaeology.

We should say at the outset that it is quite as sensible for readers to start our book at the end as at the beginning. Indeed those who read our book in Jerusalem, or who know the city well already, might do best to visit the ancient city with us in Chapter 5 before turning to Chapter 1.

At least the end-point demarcated in our title is unambiguous. The year 200 BCE was almost the midpoint of the Greek or Hellenistic period – midway between Alexander's passage down the Levantine coast to be hailed as Egypt's Pharaoh, before striking east to become Persia's Great King, and the arrival of the Roman world in the person of Pompey. In terms of local Hellenistic history, it was also close to 200 that responsibility for Jerusalem and the surrounding area passed from Alexander's Ptolemaic successors in Egypt to his Seleucid successors in Syria. The period we describe is the one reflected in the writings we know as the Hebrew Scriptures, or TaNaKh, or Old Testament. By 200 these had largely taken the forms in which we know them, even if they had not yet been collected and arranged in the different ways with which we are familiar.

However, the boundaries of Jerusalem down to 200 are not so easily defined. Are we writing about the archaeology of today's extended municipality bearing the name 'Jerusalem'? Or are we studying what was called 'Jerusalem' up until 200 BCE? And how far did that extend? Was 'Jerusalem' merely the name of a walled city or citadel, or of a compact inhabited area, or of a population centre ringed with its graveyards and, even further out, surrounded by its cultivated lands? But even to be asking such questions is already to have started the discussion . . . .

1

Orientation

Jerusalem is *the* city of the Bible. It is far from being the oldest town in Palestine, though admittedly its origins are still less than clear. Its mound of ancient ruins is less extensive than many a *tell* in that land. And by several standards it was less important than other cities of the wider 'biblical world'. But Jerusalem is *the* city of the Bible.

Unlike many of its rivals and contemporaries in the land of the Bible and beyond, Jerusalem has had an unbroken history of occupation from the time of the Bible to the present day, and under its original biblical and even pre-biblical name – although the Romans insisted on Aelia Capitolina for a period after Hadrian (135 CE), and Muslims tend to call the whole city *bayt al-maqdis* ('house of the sanctuary') or *al-quds* for short, which really refers only to its most prominent feature, rather than use the city's ancient name. It has been a principal focus of piety, prayer, and pilgrimage for Jews, Christians, and Muslims all over the world – and intermittently a focus of conflict between them. The fact that its name features, as the New Jerusalem, in biblical hopes and expectations for the end of time only underscores the focal significance of this city as a potent symbol. Yet, though we have to disentangle many later notions from the ideas of the biblical period itself, Jerusalem already then was the centre and focus of its land and people. Jerusalem was *the* city of the Bible.

The medieval Greeks must have called their capital, officially Constantinople, simply 'the city'; for its present Turkish name Istanbul continues that Greek (nick)name in scarcely disguised form. Similarly, when the Book of Lamentations begins (Lam 1:1)

How lonely sits the city that was full of people!

How like a widow has she become, she that was great among the nations! readers of the Bible know instinctively which city is being lamented. We do not need to wait for talk, several lines later, about the roads to Zion mourning or the majesty departing from the daughter of Zion to find clues to the identity of this widow-city.

Jerusalem may be by far the most familiar name among biblical cities. It may also have been quite the most intensively studied of all the cities of the biblical world. And yet we remain remarkably ignorant of much we might expect by now to know. There are two plain reasons for this unhappy state of affairs:

(a) Many individual features of the city are mentioned in the Bible; but no comprehensive account of the city is ever offered there – it was too familiar to the first readers to require description. The earliest descriptive piece available to us even a few paragraphs long is from Josephus of the later 1st century CE – the Jewish rebel general turned historian for a Roman readership. Yet his account of David's city of 1,000 years earlier is not so much a straightforward resource we can call on as one of the problems we have to face. And one wonders, when the Book of Acts speaks in much the same period of David's tomb (2:29), if it is any better informed. We have to remember that many of the biblical records, though earlier than Josephus, are still far from contemporary with what they describe. Added to that, we are not even always confident in our translation of some of the more important of these Hebrew texts (see below on the 'waterspout' and the 'blind and lame' of 2 Sam 5:8).

(b) The continuous occupation of the city means that redevelopment has also been continuous since biblical times. On the one hand its more ancient remains have been disturbed by later developments, and on the other, archaeologists have only piecemeal access to them amid the structures and needs of ongoing municipal life. As we shall find, this problem is especially acute in the most sacred area of the city.

It is the business of this volume to report on the history of investigation of Jerusalem, and to summarise what we do and do not (and in some cases cannot) know. Even though we are confining ourselves in this book to the Jerusalem of the Hebrew Scriptures, of the Christian Old Testament, and looking no further than say 200 BCE, we must still restrict ourselves to mentioning only a representative selection of the more significant studies.

Two classic works deserve immediate mention. George Adam Smith, Scottish academic and churchman, and still after almost a century the undisputed doyen of biblical geographers because of his *Historical Geography of the Holy Land* (1894), had his two volumes on *Jerusalem, from the Earliest Times to 70 A.D.* published in 1907 and 1908. Smith's work is an ongoing discussion with researchers of many nations, and represents a monument to 19th century study of Jerusalem. At more than 1100 pages, it might appear a daunting read. But be warned! It would be hard to read his haunting 25 page introduction, entitled 'The Essential City', without coming under his spell – and very unwise to ignore that chapter simply to avoid the danger of being charmed! The other

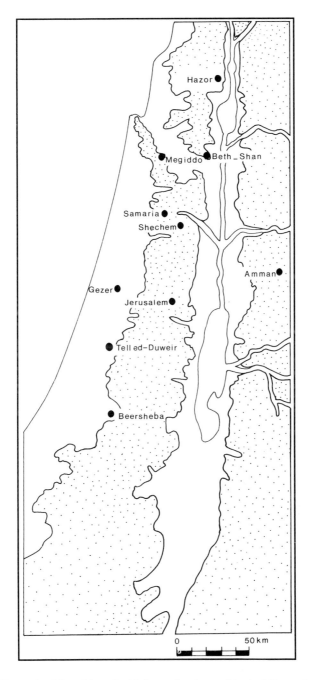

Figure 1   Map of Israel with Jerusalem located in the hill country.

classic is from a generation later – and our choice has nothing to do with the fact that we ourselves hale from the Netherlands and from Scotland: the monumental volume by Jan Simons, which set the scene for renewed investigation of the city after the Second World War: *Jerusalem in the Old Testament: Researches and Theories* (1952). And alongside them two more recent productions should be noted. *Jerusalem, the Holy City. A Bibliography* by Purvis (1988) provides details of nearly 6,000 studies of which some two-fifths relate to the period on which we are reporting. And King has contributed the long article on Jerusalem in the *Anchor Bible Dictionary* (1992).

Location

The mountains of Israel, heartland of the ancient Israelite kingdoms, are formed by a limestone massif 700-1000 m. high (Figure 1). In antiquity the southern part was a rather inaccessible, rugged area with steep valley slopes. Because of this steepness large-scale agriculture became possible only after extensive terracing had been executed in the later Iron Age. In earlier periods only dry farming could be achieved on the fertile red soils immediately along the wadis. A rainfall of about 500 mm. yearly allowed for a natural vegetation of oak, terebinth and maquis (shrubs). It was in this rather marginal region that ancient Jerusalem was located, in a lower 'saddle' between the higher Ephraim mountains to the north and the Judaean mountains to the south.

The Old City of Jerusalem is built on two ridges, the south-eastern hill and the western hill (Figure 2), bounded by the Kidron valley on the east side and the Hinnom valley on the west and south sides. West of the city several wadis lead to the more accessible Shephelah region, while the Wadi Qilt runs through the Judaean Desert east of Jerusalem to Jericho, from where it is possible to cross the river Jordan and reach the East Bank. Already in antiquity a road over the mountain plateau connected Hebron in the south with Shechem in the north, bypassing Jerusalem, which was thus situated near a crossroad formed by the north-south and east-west routes.

History of excavations

Maybe we should salute Empress Helena as the first 'archaeologist' working in Jerusalem. When she came to live in the city at the beginning of the 4th century CE, she identified the holy places of the gospels and built several memorial churches, such as the Rotunda over the Holy Sepulchre. Unlike more recent practitioners, she was able to claim divine inspiration. There are similar medieval Jewish legends about the finding of David's tomb on the south-western

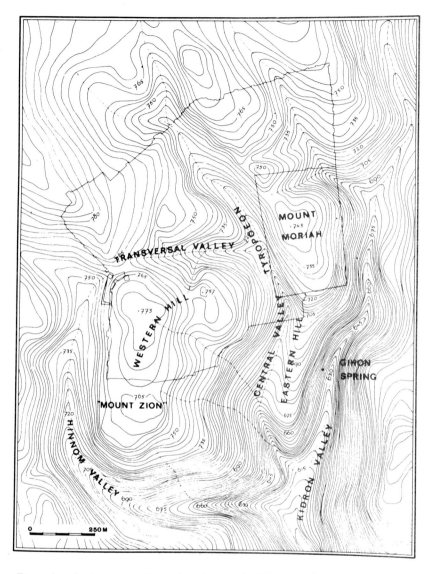

Figure 2   Contour map of Jerusalem showing the hills and valleys in and around the present-day city.

5

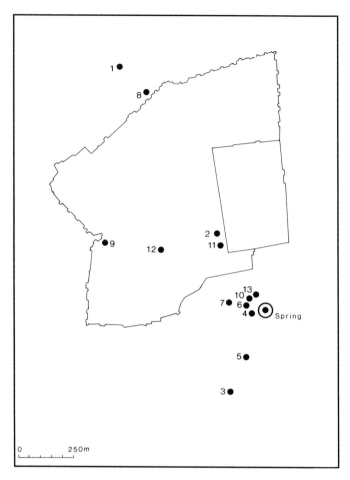

Figure 3   Main excavations executed in and around the city.

1. F. De Saulcy (1863)	7. J.W. Crowfoot (1927-28)
2. Ch. Warren (1867-70)	8. R.W. Hamilton (1931, 1937-38)
3. F.J. Bliss & A.C. Dickie (1894-97)	9. C.N. Johns (1934-40)
4. M. Parker (1909-11)	10. K.M. Kenyon (1961-67)
5. R. Weill (1913-14, 1923-24)	11. B. Mazar (1968-77)
6. R.A.S. Macalister (1923-25)	12. N. Avigad (1969-78)
	13. Y. Shiloh (1978-85)

Figure 4   *Charles Wilson digging shafts to explore the terrace wall of the al-Ḥaram al Sharif, the temple mount. These shafts are still visible today in 'Wilson's arch', located north of the Western Wall.*

hill that is now called 'Mount Zion'. It was only at the beginning of the 19th century that scholars started to doubt the authenticity of these and other holy places. Much of the early research in Jerusalem, be it the identifications of E. Robinson (1838), the survey of Ch. Wilson (1867-68) or the excavations of F. de Saulcy (1863 and 1865), Ch. Warren (1867-70) and F.J. Bliss and A.C. Dickie (1894-97), was meant to prove or disprove theories about the location of the temple of Solomon or the tombs of the kings of Judah, the identification of Golgotha (or Calvary), and the course of the ancient city walls. The story of these pioneers, as of more recent excavators in Jerusalem, has often been told in greater detail than is appropriate here (Figure 3). A fuller and well-documented recent account has been made available by King (1992).

Excavating in those earlier days meant digging underground, in tunnels and shafts, a method developed in Jerusalem to overcome two difficulties: working in a densely populated city and the prohibitions of the Ottoman authorities against approaching Muslim sanctuaries. However, it was a technique with which Wilson and Warren at least were professionally familiar, for they were 'sappers' – military engineers. This method was practised little elsewhere in the country, and even when there was no need for it, tunnelling remained in use as a Jerusalem speciality (Figure 4). Thus Bliss and Dickie, excavating in the relatively empty southern part of the city, still worked completely underground. Their work gave the first indications that the town of early biblical times had been located not within the modern city walls, but on the south-eastern hill. They were able to follow a complicated system of fortifications that surrounded this hill and which they dated to Solomon's times. Although later research showed that these walls probably belonged to the Byzantine period, the idea of the extramural location of the old town had been firmly established. Tunnelling was also the chosen method of M. Parker (1909-11) in his attempt to find the treasury of the Solomonic Temple. His expedition, otherwise of less scholarly repute, did have authoritative mapping assistance from L.H. Vincent (1911) of the École Biblique.

This led to the next phase of archaeological research, the exposure of large areas outside the walls to fill in the ground plan of ancient Jerusalem. The excavations of R. Weill (1913-14 and 1923-25) and R.A.S. Macalister (1923-24) on the south-eastern hill revealed many buildings and fortifications, the dating of which remained problematic as it was based more on information from the Bible than on an analysis of the excavated pottery – a method pioneered in Palestine at the end of previous century by Flinders Petrie. Although the excavators were familiar with this method, they considered the stratigraphy of Jerusalem's soil too confused to yield any results.

After 1925, no further large-scale excavations were conducted. The period of the grand excavations was over for the time being; and research concentrated on specific sites within the city using modern methods like deep trenching and careful small-scale excavation. J.W. Crowfoot dug a trench on the western slope of the southeastern hill (1927-28) where he found a magnificent gate house, dated by him to the period of the Jebusites. A cache of several hundred Maccabean coins was found on the floor of this building or somewhere nearby (information on the exact find spot is not very definite), so the gate is now usually assigned to the Hellenistic period, although an older dating is by no means impossible. R.W. Hamilton excavated immediately north of the Damascus Gate in 1937-38 where he uncovered an older Roman gateway, and C.N. Johns started digging in the Citadel near the Jaffa Gate (1934-40). Josephus had already described how King Herod had built a palace there with the three famous towers, Hippicus, Phasael and Mariamne. By a careful stratigraphical approach Johns was able to confirm this date, thus proving by the way that Josephus could be relied upon for the later periods he described. Most of the problems concerning the city of early biblical times were not solved, however, and the debate continued in the form of an ingenious re-analysis of existing evidence combined with new research into Bible texts.

It was only in 1961 that large-scale excavations started again under the direction of Kathleen M. Kenyon and Père Roland de Vaux. Kenyon described her reason to start working in Jerusalem as follows: 'When the British School of Archaeology in Jerusalem completed in 1958 its excavations at Jericho, it had the not very easy task of deciding what should be the next site it would tackle. Jericho had been such a success that there was a risk that work at any other place would be bathos. Jerusalem seemed to be the only other site that in importance could compete with Jericho.' Kenyon's idea was to apply the Wheeler-Kenyon method of careful stratigraphical research, that had been so successful at Jericho, to Jerusalem's complicated situation. She was confident that it would be possible thus to solve every unsolved riddle once and for all. Therefore she dug small squares all over the city, for these riddles concerned quite unrelated problems:

Why was the entrance to Jerusalem's ancient water shaft located outside the contemporary city walls?

What was the chronology of the fortifications on the southeastern hill?

To what period should the extension of the ancient town over the western hill be dated?

Where exactly were the Second and Third walls mentioned by Josephus?

What was the location of King Herod's palace?

And how large was the city in Roman times?

Kenyon's findings will be described in the following chapters. She was not, as archaeologists before her had been, a 'biblical archaeologist', someone who conducts archaeological research as part of Bible studies. For her the archaeology of Palestine was a branch of general world archaeology, and its task was to enrich our knowledge of the ancient world by systematic research and strict application of scientific methods. Though she dug at famous 'biblical' sites (Samaria, Jericho, Jerusalem), Kenyon's objectives were not specifically biblical, but rather historical in a broad sense.

Unfortunately these excavations, which continued till 1967, did not end the controversies. Although some problems had been satisfactorily solved, the debate went on as before. The weaknesses of Kenyon's way of digging – in small squares with little attention to architectural units, with the constant use of the *pars pro toto* principle ('if I don't find it in this small area, it doesn't exist at all') – were fully revealed in Jerusalem's churned-up soils. So for instance the important question of when the city started to expand over the western hill remained unsettled (see chapter 2).

After the Arab-Israeli war of 1967, several large-scale excavations as well as many smaller ones were conducted in Jerusalem by Israeli archaeologists, who now had access to the ancient parts of the city. With the permission of the Islamic Auqaf authorities, Benjamin Mazar excavated a large area west and south of the Temple Mount (1968-77), a site strictly *haram* ('forbidden') in earlier times. He found extensive architectural remains of the Herodian, Roman, Byzantine and early Islamic periods, thus adding important chapters to the (archaeological) history of the city. He even succeeded in opening up a new gate in the walls of Jerusalem, to join the seven gates that had guarded the entrance to the holy city for centuries. This is the Excavation Gate in the south wall, necessary to allow the diggers easy access to excavation squares outside the Old City wall.

Nahman Avigad explored the Jewish Quarter of the Old City (1969-78), an area that was to be rebuilt almost completely, thus allowing large scale operations. Iron Age fortifications, houses and villas from the Herodian period (with impressive evidence of the Roman attack on the city in 70 CE) and the Byzantine Cardo must be mentioned here as the most important finds of this excavation.

Yigal Shiloh tackled the south-eastern hill again (1978-85), picking up where Weill, Parker, Macalister and Kenyon had worked before. Many of his discoveries will be described in later chapters.

These excavations were characterised by excellent organisation and intensive use of technical appliances, a preference for the exposure of large areas with much attention to architecture and less to stratigraphy, and the composition of a corpus of complete pots from floors instead of the detailed analysis of sherd material. A primary aim of these Israeli excavations was the reconstruction of a visible and visitable national history, mainly from what they called the First and Second Temple periods, a measure which encompasses a little over a millennium from the Iron Age, through the Persian and Hellenistic periods, to the Herodian period. Although these excavations were an enormous success, the very quick way of digging with the help of inexperienced volunteers and the often hasty and controversial interpretations have repeatedly been criticised.

The digging may have been well-organised, and in some cases speedy; but comprehensive publication of the results has been another matter. For most excavations since 1961 properly scientific publication of the material has only recently started (e.g. Tushingham 1985; Mazar and Mazar 1989; Franken and Steiner 1990; Ariel 1990; and De Groot and Ariel 1992); and this seriously hampers our interpretation of their results. De Vaux, Kenyon, and then Shiloh all died before pre-publication study of their finds was well advanced. Nonetheless our knowledge of Jerusalem has been greatly enriched by their excavations, and a much clearer picture of its occupational history can now be presented. As has just been suggested, one of us has been closely involved for some years with work on the Kenyon material. Of course many questions remain open for debate, but even after – or should it be especially after? – 150 years of archaeological work in the city that should come as no surprise.

Jerusalem in the Hebrew Bible

Jerusalem and its physical features are mentioned and occasionally described in the biblical writings – and, much more often perhaps, merely hinted at. Such references to the city sometimes add to the archaeologists' burden, and occasionally help to explain what they find. We must now inspect more closely this second main source for Jerusalem in the period of the Hebrew Bible or Old Testament. And we do this for two reasons. One is simply so that the real nature of archaeology's conversation partner in this enterprise may become better known to us. The Bible is a very diverse collection of writings: some more literary, some more religious, some more historical. These varied written materials also require critical investigation. And the basic questions are not much different from those we put to the physical remains of the ancient city. What is their date? For what purpose were they written? Were they re-written at a later date for the same or a different purpose? The other reason for paying careful attention to these writings is that the Bible is our only means of access to some parts of ancient Jerusalem which archaeology has been unable to penetrate. Problematic or helpful, the biblical evidence must be correlated with the archaeological record as we search for the history of the city.

Among its books, Samuel-Kings and Chronicles are our main narrative sources for the period of the monarchy in Israel and Judah. These two biblical collections have a great deal of material in common; for much of the story of David and Solomon and for much of the following account of the kings of Judah, they run in broadly parallel lines. Most biblical scholars have offered the same explanation for their links since the beginning of the 19th century. They have taught that Samuel and Kings were the source, and that Chronicles was produced by a partly selective and partly expansionist re-writing of Samuel and Kings, in which many parts were omitted and much new material was added. One of us has recently urged an alternative account strongly: that the material Samuel-Kings and Chronicles both still report was also their shared source (Auld 1994). On this view, neither the authors of Samuel-Kings nor those of Chronicles made large omissions from this common source that had told the 400-year story of the kings of Jerusalem from David around 1000 BCE to the deportations to Babylon in the two decades after 600 BCE. Both repeated it in full. Each gave the fuller story they produced its own distinctive stamp, not by what they left out, but by the large-scale developments and additions they both made to the common source material.

11

If Auld is right to detect the same source material re-used in both familiar biblical books, this has implications for our other leading questions: date and purpose? We have to detach – and just occasionally reconstruct – the oldest available story of Jerusalem's kings from the two alternative settings in which we read it now. Once that is done, we get some leverage on its date; for even the common source must belong to the period after the deportation of Judah's last king, because it already tells that whole story. And so our biblical books of Samuel-Kings and Chronicles, which share this post-collapse source, must be still later; both of them in fact from well into the 'Second Temple' period.

The purpose of the successor books can then be detected by comparing each with the other and also with the source. Chronicles is much the more optimistic of the two. It portrays David and Solomon as ideal rulers from a Golden Age at the birth of the dynasty. Each successor king is a responsible agent who reaps the due reward from his behaviour; and yet each unsatisfactory king is also able to repent. Chronicles also takes a strong interest in the cultic arrangements and the precise responsibilities of priestly and levitical clans, which we also find reflected in the headings and musical directions of many of the Psalms.

Whether we describe Samuel-Kings by contrast as more pessimistic or more realistic may tell more about ourselves than about these biblical books. Kings blames the kings of Judah – from the beginnings to the end, and with remark-ably few exceptions – for the collapse. Its source had praised many of the kings, and this judgement was left unchanged in Chronicles. But the Book of Kings often qualifies and limits the favourable judgement. It interleaves with the old story of Judah alone, the fatal two-hundred-year story of its sister nation Israel to the north; and blames Judah and her kings for not drawing appro-priate lessons from observing that tragedy. It adds substantially to the reports in its source about David and Solomon. In that source and in Chronicles too, David and Solomon were portrayed as the founder kings from an ideal age. They had made Jerusalem the nation's capital, had built houses there for their god and for themselves; and they had grown rich, with the support of the merchant king Hiram of Tyre from the Lebanese coast to the north, and to the admiration of the Queen of Sheba from the exotic south. However, the open-ing chapters of Kings add to their source on Solomon a number of passages where disapproval of his actions is made quite explicit, and others where Solomon's responsibility for the royal line's ultimate collapse is clearly implied. Compared with Kings, the Book of Samuel seems both less and more radical at the same time; it does not actually state in so many words that David had been responsible for what was to follow, but it portrays David as a towering tragic figure of flawed greatness. The older common source had made plain that the divine promise to Jerusalem and David did come with conditions; 2 Samuel and Kings added evidence that these conditions were immediately breached.

Jerusalem makes a very early appearance in the common source. As soon as all Israel had made David king at Hebron on Saul's death, David made an immediate move on Jerusalem. Yet its short report of what takes place there raises more questions than it answers:

> And the king and his men went to Jerusalem against the Jebusite(s). And he (they) said to David, 'You shall not come here'. And David took the stronghold of Zion – that is the city of David. And David said, 'Whoever strikes the Jebusite [first will become head and leader; and Joab son of Zeruiah went up first and become head]. And David lived in the fortress, and it was named city of David. And David (re-)built round about from the Millo.

In these very few verses (2 Sam 5:6-9 or 1 Chron 11:4-8) several familiar names are clustered. Though well known, they remain hard to define precisely: Jerusalem, the Jebusite(s), Zion, the city of David, and the Millo. We start our review of these names with the last.

The '**Millo**', which could be the Hebrew for the 'Fill', and which according to this short report David built or rebuilt after his takeover of the city, makes only this one solitary appearance in all of the common source from David to the Babylonian destruction of his city. 1 Kings adds three mentions of this feature as being one of Solomon's several constructions too – in 9:15,24; and in 11:27; but none of these is repeated within 2 Chron 1-9. 1 Kings 11:27 reports most fully of the three that Solomon 'built the Millo, closed the breach of the city of David'. These three references to Solomon against only one to David have encouraged some scholars to give Solomon the benefit of any historical doubt – and to suggest that the story of David's move on Jerusalem is anachronistic in its closing words. But that seems a fragile argument: this David story in Samuel is confirmed in Chronicles, while that book gives no backing at all to what Kings says about Solomon and the Millo. Much later in 2 Kings 12:20 King Joash is assassinated 'in the house of Millo' (*byt ml'* in Hebrew), though the parallel in 2 Chron 24:25 offers 'on his bed' ('*l mṭṭw* in Hebrew). If the Kings version is correct here, we might compare this component of Jerusalem with a similar feature in Shechem according to Judg 9:6,20. There is also extra-biblical information in R.C. Steiner (1989).

In the common source, there is very seldom any mention of the **Jebusite(s)**. The Hebrew name is actually singular. It is normally understood as a collective, and so translated as an English plural referring to the inhabitants of the city or area; but it could also be read as a singular referring to the individual who held the throne of the city, or of a city state that included the surrounding area. The next reference to the Jebusite in the common source after the story of David's move on the city encourages this singular/collective approach. In 2 Sam 24:16,18 (or 1 Chron 21:15,18), the Jerusalemite from whom David purchases the 'threshing floor' where the temple is to be built is Araunah 'the Jebusite' (possibly the former ruler). Lastly the Jebusite(s) finds mention in 1 Kings 9:20 (or 2 Chron 8:7) among other previous rulers or peoples whom Solomon presses into service for his construction works – projects which do not in Chronicles include the Millo. The name 'Jebus' itself is very much rarer in the Bible than 'the Jebusite(s)', being found only in Judg 19:10-11 and 1 Chron 11:4-5. Whether it was originally an alternative name for Jerusalem, or whether it belonged originally to a neighbouring locality such as the modern suburb of Shu'fat (Miller 1974: 126), or whether it has been derived secondarily from the name of the people, is hotly debated.

Zion is a name found frequently in the poetry of the Psalms and the Prophets, but very rarely elsewhere in the Bible. It is mentioned within this shared narrative source only here at the beginning and in one other context. 2 Sam 5:7 tells us that David 'took the stronghold of Zion, that is the city of David' (and 5:9 goes on to report that he 'dwelt in the stronghold and called it the city of David'). The other mention is in 1 Kings 8:1, where Solomon moves the Ark 'out of the city of David, which is Zion' to his new temple. In the first shared reference, Zion – or at least its stronghold – is equated with 'the city of David'; in the other, this 'city of David' is equated with Zion. If we are unsure what exactly Zion means, can we be any more certain about the other name? What precisely was 'the city of David' with which Zion was equated?

Every king of Judah from David to Ahaz – a period of over two hundred years – was buried 'in the **city of David**'. In fact, throughout the common source, no king is noted as being buried elsewhere: Chronicles, and therefore the material it shares with Kings, makes no mention of where the last kings of Judah, from Hezekiah onwards, were interred. Was 'city of David' simply an alternative name for Jerusalem, in honour of the king who had acquired it for Israel? Was it the old core of a city which later grew: the original city as David took it? Was 'stronghold of Zion' a name for the whole older city he took, or only of its fortress which became renamed 'city of David'? Or did 'city of David' refer more precisely to that part of Jerusalem which contained the royal necropolis, or at least the former royal necropolis? It has been noted that there is no other evidence of Iron Age burials within walled cities. However, we may presume that kings, as 'sons of God' were not subject to such normal restrictions.

Apart from the regular references over centuries to royal burials, there are only two other shared mentions of 'city of David': 2 Sam 6:12 (cf 1 Chron 15:29) tells of David bringing the Ark after its liberation from the Philistines to the 'city of David'; and 1 Kings 9:24 (cf 2 Chron 8:11) tells how Solomon brought up the daughter of Pharaoh from the 'city of David to her own house which Solomon had built for her'. Neither of these memories helps our main question: both the Ark and the Egyptian princess could have been lodged in the fortress. Royal burials might also have been arranged there. (Kings adds two further references, each related to passages we have already mentioned: 1 Kings 3:1 has Solomon bringing Pharaoh's daughter there on their marriage, till his building work in Jerusalem was complete; and 1 Kings 11:27 portrays Jeroboam as forced labour overseer for Solomon who 'built the Millo, and closed the breach of the city of David his father'. Indeed that note leaves its reader wondering whether two separate projects of Solomon were in the writer's mind, or whether Solomon closed the breach *by* building the Millo. 2 Chron 32:5,30 and 33:14 report fresh fortifications relating to the 'city of David' – 32:5 has Hezekiah strengthening 'the Millo of the city of David'. The only other references to this feature are the related Neh 3:15 and 12:37, and Is 22:9 within a larger passage that describes defensive work in time of threat.)

So much for some of **Jerusalem's** features or at least some alternative names. The six letters of Jerusalem's own name in Hebrew most likely spell the composite name *yrw-šlm*, to be interpreted as 'the foundation/establishment of Shalem'. Shalem was a god known from the traditions of the ancient Levant, and may have been referred to in the introduction of Melchizedek in Genesis 14:18. So much for the name itself. But what did it convey in the Hebrew Bible period? We think of it as the capital of Judah. Yet legally it seems to have been also an entity distinct from Judah, for we often read about 'Judah and Jerusalem' or 'Jerusalem and Judah'. Just as each king of Judah till Ahaz was buried 'in the city of David', so every king of Judah from David to the final collapse was said to have 'reigned in Jerusalem'. Most of the other mentions of its name are similarly formal, referring to comings and goings. Was Jerusalem just the built-up and fortified royal residence and headquarters – and shrine? How much territory round about it bore this name? And what sorts of settlement and occupation might the Bible lead us to expect?

The feature of Jerusalem's architecture that recurs most frequently in the common text was not part of the city David took over. The 'house of Yahweh' is the normal biblical expression for what we tend to call the Temple of Solomon. 'Temple' conveys to the modern western mind first and foremost a place for religious worship. However, like other prominent or national temples of its time, the Jerusalem temple functioned quite as much as a bank or treasury as it did as a sanctuary – and we should remember that the great altar for public sacrifice was outside, not inside. The temple was plundered by Shishak of Egypt in the reign of Rehoboam; by Baasha and Jehoash of Israel in the reigns of Asa and Amaziah; then finally by Nebuchadnezzar of Babylon in the reign of Jehoiachin. This 'house' is mentioned most repeatedly at that point in Judah's royal story where the continuity of the line of David was most endangered. At the death of King Ahaziah, his mother Athaliah usurped power and attempted to destroy the royal family. Joash, son of the dead king Ahaziah, was hidden in the 'house of Yahweh', in or at which he was later proclaimed king by Jehoiada the priest. The restoration of the monarchy was followed by repair work on the temple – and then a ruinous handover by Joash of the treasures from both the house of Yahweh and the king's house to Hazael of Syria who had moved against Jerusalem after taking Gath. His namesake Jehoash of Israel was shortly to sack the 'house of Yahweh' after breaking the wall from the Ephraim Gate to the Corner Gate. Jotham is later said to have 'built the Upper Gate of the house of Yahweh', though probably not as part of the necessary repair.

The 'king's house' is less often mentioned, and always as an adjunct to the 'house of Yahweh' – a place where further treasures were to be found. But one familiar name for part of the heart of old Jerusalem, prominent in modern usage, is never used in the shared text nor in fact anywhere in Samuel-Kings. [The] **Ophel**, or 'the bulge' or 'the hill', is found in two prophetic texts – Is 32:14 and Mic 4:8 – and then only in late prose texts: in addition to the shared text in 2 Chron 27:3; 33:14; and in Neh 3:26-7; 11:21 where it is the hill on which the temple servants reside. Finally, in terms of buildings, the prophetess Huldah lived with her husband, who was a high official in the time of Josiah, in the 'Second Quarter'.

A Walled City?

It is the late biblical book of Nehemiah which offers the richest information about Jerusalem in the final two or three centuries under our review. And that is also the book which tells us most about the city's walls and gates and towers. It reports a visit 'to the city of his fathers' tombs' by the cupbearer to King Artaxerxes, with the king's permission to rebuild it: first a secret nocturnal inspection (2:11-16), then the rebuilding (3:1-32), and finally the dedicatory procession (12:31-43). It is the second of these portions which is quite the most detailed, though there is evidence that it has suffered some accidental loss. Yet, typical of our biblical sources, it raises quite as many questions as it answers. Understanding all its detail is impossible at our distance: as we have remarked about other texts, it was written for readers who knew the city in a way that we do not.

16

Nehemiah 3 describes, section by section, the restoration of Jerusalem as a walled city. Each section of the wall was the responsibility of priests, or notables and their men, or guilds. Sometimes it is reported that these were rebuilding the section close to their own property. And at other times it may be assumed that builders had an interest in their section: like the priests at the north end of the temple (3:1), and so possibly the goldsmiths also near its eastern perimeter (3:31-32). We shall note more fully in chapter 3 that the Temple functioned also as a bank. Nehemiah 3 describes the restoration of Jerusalem as a walled city, but not the rebuilding of the previous walls. Nehemiah's walls bounded a Jerusalem reduced both on the east side and the west: on the east, the new walls were higher up the hill than the ancient ones, and, to the west, the late monarchic expansion (the *Mishneh*) was excluded (Williamson 1984).

The reported repair work begins and ends (3:1,32) with the Sheep Gate and moves anti-clockwise round the new wall. The Sheep Gate (also 12:39) was to the north, suitably close to the Temple, probably at the east end of the short north wall which required the extra protection of the Tower of the Hundred and the Tower of Hananel (both also 3:1; 12:39). The next four gates listed are to the west: the Fish Gate (3:3 – also 12:39) was in the north-west; next came the 'Old City' Gate (3:6); between that and the Valley Gate (3:13; also 2:13,15) was the Tower of the 'Ovens' (also 12:38); and finally, the Refuse or Dung Gate (3:13,14 – also 2:14; 12:31), which by all accounts was near the lowest and southern most end of the city. Also at the south end, doubtless close to the present Pool of Siloam, was the Spring Gate (3:15 – also 2:13; 12:37). What we have translated the 'Old City' Gate is often called the 'Old' Gate, but the Hebrew is then problematical. The Hebrew is sometimes emended to give the Mishneh Gate. Either way, this was probably the gate which had once led from the older part of town to the new or 'second' (Hebrew *Mishneh*) quarter, which had been built up gradually and then defended in the later monarchic period. The emendation and the translation we have offered simply look at the same gate from opposite sides. The description in Nehemiah 3 is quite explicit that each of the six gates so far mentioned, from the Sheep Gate round to the Spring Gate, was itself repaired as part of the repair of Jerusalem's walls.

Moving northwards again up the east side, we find mention first of the Water Gate (3:26 – also 12:37), almost certainly in the vicinity of the Gihon water-source; then of the Horses Gate (3:28), the East Gate (3:29), and the Watch Gate (3:31). However, none of these is said to have been repaired by Nehemiah's colleagues. Was there less damage on the east side of Jerusalem? Or is it more probable that some or all of these eastern names refer to gates in the earlier now damaged and abandoned east wall – and that it was inside and higher up the hill from the old wall that Nehemiah built his? If this is a fair reading of the text, then we are receiving information in the one report about different periods. That may help to explain the mention of an Ephraim Gate on the west side. It had been an older gate on a nearby but different line. People mustered and made booths there on the feast of Tabernacles (8:16), just as they did in the open space by the Water Gate to the east (8:1,3,16). The dedicatory procession moved past it up the west side (12:39); but it is not one of the gates listed as repaired in chapter 3. That procession, having rounded the two northern towers and the Sheep Gate, came to a halt at the Gate of the Guard – probably an alternative name for the Watch Gate (3:31). Since the two processions end with their leaders in the Temple, at least that gate must have given access through the eastern wall.

Traditions linger in a city like Jerusalem. The Watch Gate, or Gate of the Guard, in whose vicinity the goldsmiths were responsible for the repairs, had been close to the present Golden Gate. And the Horses Gate cannot have been far distant from the current south-east corner of the *Haram* (the Muslim name for the sacred, literally 'forbidden', area), just inside which we find what tradition calls Solomon's stables. The rather more difficult question we have to face now is how to work backwards from this uniquely comprehensive text in Nehemiah: how to correlate all the less comprehensive biblical reports about earlier periods with the gates and towers Nehemiah mentions, whether rebuilt or not.

The narratives in the Book of Jeremiah tell of the period just before and after the great calamity, but were composed in a later period. Several of them mention gates of Jerusalem; but only the Horses Gate, which appears in Jer 31:38-40 along with the Tower of Hananel and some other features, bears a name familiar from Nehemiah. The others are the Corner Gate (from that same passage), the Potsherd Gate (19:2), the (Upper) Benjamin Gate (of/to the house of the Lord) (20:2; 37:13; 38:7), the New Gate of/to the house of the Lord (26:10; 36:10), the Middle Gate (39:3), and 'the gate between two walls towards the King's Garden' (39:4; 52:7).

We have to consider which of these names may be alternatives for names used in Nehemiah, and which might even be alternatives for each other. Still today, many of the gates in what is now called the 'Old City' of Jerusalem are known by at least three names: what is widely known in English as the Damascus Gate is called the Gate of the Pillar in Arabic, and Shechem Gate in Hebrew.

(a) The Benjamin or Upper Gate is closely associated with the Temple. We do not know whether in this period the Temple had its own named gates giving access to its own courts. We prefer to assume that this was a city gate that gave immediate access to the Temple; and was the north-eastern gate which Nehemiah calls the Sheep Gate.

(b) The Corner Gate appears in Jer 31:38-40 as a cardinal point to the west within a promise of restoration that offers a short conspectus of the whole perimeter of the city:

... the city shall be rebuilt ... from the Tower of Hananel to the Corner Gate.
... straight to the Hill Gareb, and then turn to Goah.
The whole valley of the dead bodies and ashes, and all the fields as far as Kidron,
to the corner of the Horse Gate toward the east ...

Near the end of the prophecy of Zechariah (14:10), a similar prediction mentions two of the same features:

from the Gate of Benjamin to the place of the former gate, to the Corner Gate,
and from the Tower of Hananel to the king's wine presses.

Here the second line appears to mean from north to south, in which case the first may signify east to west, though the gates mentioned are east and west of the Temple, and so north-east and north-west of the city as a whole.

(c) The New Gate (Jer 26:10; 36:10) was also in the vicinity of the Temple.

(d) The Potsherd Gate (Jer 19:2) is associated with the exit towards the Valley of Hinnom, and so is probably either Nehemiah's Valley Gate or his Refuse Gate.

(e) The Middle Gate (39:3) cannot be located, unless it be the same as (f).

(f) The gate between the two walls . . . , by which the desperate breakout was made from the Babylonian encirclement, was perhaps Nehemiah's Spring Gate (Neh 3:15), by the Pool of Siloam and the King's Garden.

Our question about whether all the gates of which we read were in the perimeter wall of the city, or whether there were also inner walls for temple or palace, reappears as we try to translate and locate Queen Athaliah's violent death as reported a little differently in 2 Kings 11:16; 2 Chron 23:15. Jehoiada the priest gave instructions that she should not be killed 'in the house of the Lord'. Accordingly, she was taken 'to[wards] the horses' entrance to the king's house, and there she was slain'. Since it is unlikely there was horse traffic between temple and palace, we assume that she was taken to or near to the Horses Gate, naturally a larger gate which gave immediate access to the palace, to be killed.

Was the extent of Jerusalem always defined by its walls? And did people in all periods 'leave' Jerusalem by passing through its gates? What are we to make of the fact that Jerusalem's gates are mentioned in much greater number in texts about the later biblical period than about earlier times – and that it is only in a late text that the watercourse called Kidron is actually said to be 'outside Jerusalem'? The Kidron is mentioned only once in the source-material common to Samuel-Kings and Chronicles: Asa burned there the image his mother had made for Asherah. Did the Kidron mark the boundary of Jerusalem? In the common text as reflected in 1 Kings 15:13 and 2 Chron 15:16, Asa cut down his mother Maacah's image, 'and burned it at the brook Kidron'. Should we expect that that happened outside the city? In similar fashion, doubtless inspired by the original Asa account, the Chronicler's extended report of Hezekiah's cultic reforms (2 Chron 29:16; 30:14) uses unspecific language, of Kidron as simply the valley to which unwelcome sacral material was removed. By contrast, Kings' extended account of Josiah's reform (2 Kings 23:4-20) twice states quite precisely (vv.4,6) that the Kidron where cultic implements for Asherah and Baal were burned was 'outside Jerusalem'. Then, back to the earlier period, one story each about David (2 Sam 15:13) and Solomon (1 Kings 2:37), implies that to cross the Kidron was to leave Jerusalem. The only other biblical mention is within Jer 31:38-40 which anticipates an extended reconstruction of Jerusalem including 'the fields as far as the brook Kidron'.

As we noted above, the only gates that appear in the shared source for the monarchic period – itself a document only written down after the collapse – are in the northern, upper half of the city: Jehoash of Israel broke the wall between Ephraim and Corner Gates, and went on to sack the 'house of Yahweh'; and the 'Upper Gate of/to the house of Yahweh', which Jotham later built was also in the north wall – Ezek 9:2 says so, and we have noted that Jer 20:2 associates it with the Benjamin Gate. But did these walls and gates protect the whole city – or simply its fortified 'acropolis' that lay to the north of the residential area? Much of that acropolis lies under the *Haram* and is unavailable for excavation. The Bible gives no clear answer about the extent of its southern fortifications in the various phases of the period of Judah's kings. For that we do need to turn back to archaeology.

2

Jerusalem's Development

For most of its ancient history Jerusalem was not located within the boundaries of the present-day 'Old City', but to the south of it, on a small spur of hill, which is now once again called the City of David. King David himself would surely not recognise it, because in his days even the landscape looked different. The Kidron valley was about 15 metres deeper, and the slope of the hill was much steeper and difficult to climb. The road along the houses was not a road at all, but a valley, called the Cheesemongers' (or Tyropoeon) valley by Josephus' time. The repeated destructions of Jerusalem have succeeded in filling up the valleys, and piling up a layer of debris more than ten metres high

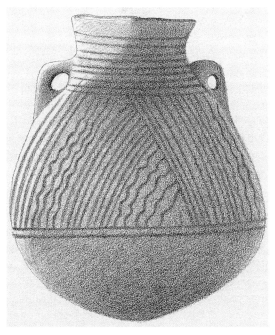

Figure 5   Juglet from the Early Bronze Age with painted decoration.

on the slopes of the hill. So much had the landscape changed, that as early as Roman times the inhabitants of Jerusalem no longer remembered where David's city had been situated. Josephus (1st century CE) located the Stronghold of Zion, taken by David, on the plateau of the western hill; here David was thought to have built his own city and his tomb, a tradition which still clings to this place which is now once again called Mount Zion.

The many large-scale excavations that have been conducted in Jerusalem since the end of the last century have demonstrated beyond doubt that it was on the south-eastern hill, near the spring Gihon, that the ancient city was built. In the Kidron valley, beside the road that runs along it, a small house hides the entrance to the spring, the most important source of water for the ancient town. A staircase now leads down to the spring itself through metres of debris; but once upon a time its water sprang freely from the side of the hill, making its surroundings green and lush. The mountains around Jerusalem were not terraced and farmed then, but their fertile red soils were covered with oak and terebinth; and the wadis, now dry, once transported the run-off water from the mountains during the rainy season. That was how Jerusalem looked to the first people who came to settle there permanently in the Middle Bronze Age, around 1800 BCE.

The Bronze Age

From earlier periods few archaeological remains have been found, mainly tombs in natural or man-made caves. No permanent settlement was ever built near the spring Gihon before the Middle Bronze Age; the area was the domain of (semi-)nomadic pastoralists who visited the spring and buried their dead in its vicinity; in antiquity religious importance was often attached to springs. The oldest tombs date from the first part of the Early Bronze Age (ca. 3000 BCE) and contained the beautiful red painted pottery typical of that period (Figure 5; Vincent 1911, plates IX, X). Analysis of the pottery showed that it was made of clay found in different regions in Palestine, confirming the idea that these were the graves of wandering herdsmen. A small building was discovered some 100 m. south of the spring, consisting of one room with benches along the walls (Shiloh 1984, 11-12). This may have been a small shrine, but further identification has to await its publication. The Early Bronze Age had been a period of extensive urbanisation in Palestine and the hill country was dotted with villages and towns. The question may be asked here why Jerusalem was not settled then. With its spring and fertile soils it would have formed an attractive location for a farming community. It is possible that the spring Gihon actually constituted the obstacle, as it was difficult to use in its original form.

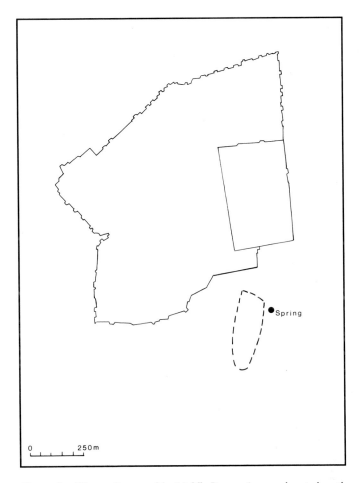

Spring

0   250m

*Figure 6   The small town of the Middle Bronze Age was located south
of the present day 'old city', near the spring Gihon.*

It is an intermittent spring; it emits a gush of water for only 40 minutes every 6-
8 hours, which would flow away over the rocks – hence its name, meaning 'the
Gusher' in Hebrew. To use it the spring had to be 'canalised': a basin had to be
cut in the rock to catch the water; and the spring's original outlet had to be
blocked, something that was apparently achieved only in later periods.

In the following Intermediate Period (2300-2000 BCE), when the urban
civilisation of the previous period had largely vanished, the land was once
again the territory of semi-nomadic tribes. These people farmed small fields in

*Figure 7   The two city walls of Jerusalem located on the steep slope of the south-
eastern hill, looking south. The lowest wall dates from ca. 1800 BCE and
curves uphill; the upper one (behind the scale) is from 700 BCE. The stone
wall, on the left of the photograph, was made by the excavators to protect
the excavation square.*

spring and moved on with their flocks to warmer areas in winter. Near Jerusalem several villages dating from this period have been found along the wadis,
but the site itself was still not settled. A cemetery with eleven shaft tombs has
been found on the Mount of Olives. However, it was only in the beginning of
the Middle Bronze Age, when a second wave of urbanisation spread over Palestine, that people began to build a town on the south-eastern hill of Jerusalem
(ca. 1800 BCE). Compared to other settlements of that period it was a small
town (Figure 6), measuring less than 5 hectares (some 12 acres), against Hazor's
84ha.; but it had a sturdy encircling wall 2 meters wide, made of large boulders
(Figure 7).

*Figure 8   Section through the water system, discovered by Charles Warren. One
(right)   tunnel was not completed, the other leads to a narrow shaft where water
could be drawn. To the right, under a modern building, sits the original
spring.*

24

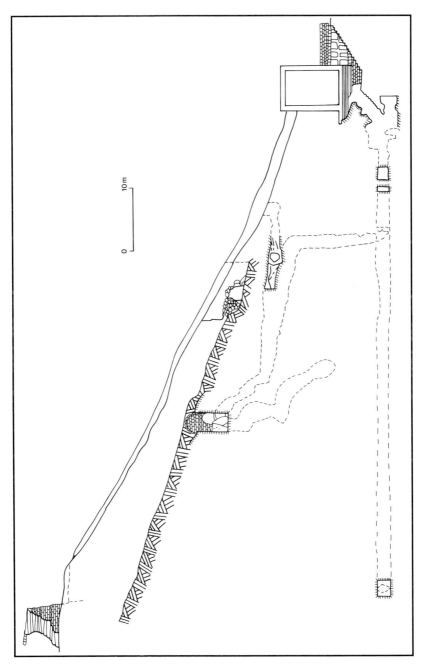

10 m

0

25

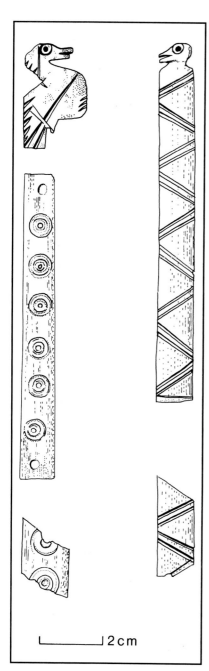

Figure 9 Decorated bone inlays dating from the Middle Bronze Age and originally attached to a wooden box [after Ariel 1990, Figure 9].

The northern boundary of the town was determined by the existence of a natural stone ridge, three metres high and running from east to west across the top of the hill. At the north side of it there is a small cross valley, traces of which were detected in Kenyon's sites H and R. The town wall was built on top of the stone ridge south of this valley, which thus formed a natural moat at the foot of the wall. Stretches of this wall have also been discovered halfway down the slope of the south-eastern hill, suprisingly leaving the spring outside the town wall. From this period must stem the first attempts to develop the spring. It is possible that the famous Warren's Shaft or Dragon Shaft was also cut then, although there is no archaeological evidence for its date. Warren's Shaft consists of an underground tunnel leading from inside the town wall to a deep, but narrow shaft; it is just possible to lower a bucket in it to draw water from a pool 14 m. below, filled from the spring by another, smaller tunnel (Figure 8). The builders of this water system no doubt utilised existing underground natural karstic clefts and tunnels (Gill 1991). The stairs of the underground tunnel are well-worn, suggesting age-long use.

We know nothing of the town itself; only fragments of houses have survived the building programmes of later times. The finds however allow some glimpses into the daily life of the settlement. More

Figure 10   The word 'Rushalimum' (Jerusalem) as written in the Egyptian Execration Texts dating from the 20th to the 18th centuries BCE.

than 50% of the pottery found consisted of large storage jars, from which we can deduce that the town had a function as a storage or market centre. This agrees with the evidence from some contemporary farming villages excavated along the wadis in the vicinity of Jerusalem. Analysis of their faunal remains shows that meat and milk were produced there mainly for a central market (Horwitz 1989). The storage jars mentioned above were all made from clay dug near these villages, which was used by local potters who sold their wares at the markets in town. Several buildings in the villages showed evidence for specialised pottery production, such as hand-driven pottery wheels, and basins to mix the clay.

Jerusalem was the centre of economic power in the region, and therefore of political, military and religious power as well. Too small to have existed on its own, it was rather the provincial outpost of a more powerful city-state. The population seems to have been rather well-to-do: coloured beads made of stones and faience have been found, and decorated bone inlays for furniture (Figure 9), suggesting specialised workshops. It is possible that only the prince/ruler of the region lived in the town itself, together with his retinue of officials, servants and soldiers. Besides a palace or governmental building the town would have housed store-buildings, a shrine or temple, and several large open spaces used as markets; it would have been able to harbour the population of the villages nearby who would take refuge in the town in times of danger, together with their flocks.

It has been suggested that the name 'Jerusalem' (in the form *Rushalimum*) was inscribed on broken pottery sherds discovered in Egypt, known as the 'Execration Texts' (Figure 10). The sherds contained the names of the enemies of Egypt, cities, peoples and rulers, and were probably broken as an act of magic: 'so will the enemies of Egypt be shattered'. These texts have been dated to the 19th or 18th centuries. However, the mention of this name cannot be used as 'proof' that Jerusalem was an important city then. The name in

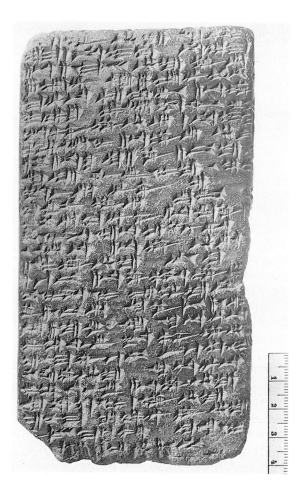

Figure 11 One of the Amarna letters written by Abdi Khiba, prince of Urusalim.

itself does not specify a town – it could as easily indicate a region or tribe. Historically it would be surprising, not to say unbelievable, to find that such a small provincial town as the Jerusalem that has been uncovered by excavation would have bothered the mighty Pharaoh of Egypt or required execration on his behalf. We do not know how long this town existed, but it cannot have been long. As far as is known – not all the evidence has been published yet – no pottery from the second half of the Middle Bronze Age has been found at all.

For reasons unknown the town ceased to exist after a mere hundred years, although the farming communities along the wadis seem to have continued to thrive until the end of the Middle Bronze Age.

If we rely on written sources, the Late Bronze Age was an important period in the history of Jerusalem. Palestine was subject to Egypt, and in the Egyptian capital of that period, el-Amarna, an archive has been discovered containing the official correspondence of Pharaoh Amenhotep III and his son Echnaton, dating from the first half of the 14th century. Some of the letters were written by the princes or rulers of Palestinian city-states such as Shechem, Gaza, Megiddo and Beth Shean. Six letters came from the prince of Urusalim, whose name was Abdi Khiba. These letters give a fascinating picture of the life and worries of this ruler, who had to pay a heavy tribute to the Pharaoh each year, consisting of slaves and concubines. He had a bad name: he frequently attacked other cities, trying to steal their land, and many princes complain about his behaviour in their letters to the Pharaoh. It is no wonder that archaeologists have tried to discover the city of Abdi Khiba. In her excavations in Jerusalem, Kathleen Kenyon found a series of stone terraces built against the slope of the south-eastern hill above the spring Gihon, which she dated to the 14th century, the Amarna-period. Analysis of the pottery has now shown that these terraces were built no earlier than the end of the 13th century – much too late to form the city Urusalim. No remains of a 14th century city have yet been discovered in any of the large-scale excavations conducted in Jerusalem, not even a sherd of pottery. Archaeologically speaking, Jerusalem was not occupied at all during the Late Bronze Age. Only a large tomb on the Mount of Olives, filled with hundreds of jars and vases from the 17th to the 14th centuries, testifies to the presence of human beings in the vicinity of the site (Saller 1964).

It seems that this is one of the many instances where written sources and archaeological evidence do not agree. As the archaeological evidence is hard to 'explain away', we must direct a fresh look at the letters Abdi Khiba has written (Figure 11). There is in the first place the possibility that Urusalim was located elsewhere in Palestine; geographical references in the letters, however, make this a very slight possibility indeed. On the other hand, if Urusalim was located in Jerusalem, then maybe it was not a large city at all. In that case we may interpret the 'lands of Urusalim' as being a royal dominion of the Pharaoh, with Abdi Khiba as his steward, who lived in a fortified house somewhere near the spring. In one of his letters Abdi Khiba complains that Nubian soldiers attacked his house, 'which was very strong', and cut a hole in its roof, whereas he never mentions the walls of his city or its strong gates, as other princes proudly do. The tomb on the Mount of Olives may have belonged to his family.

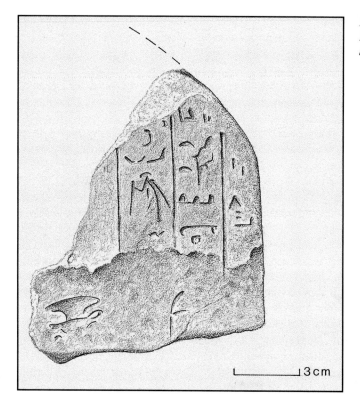

Figure 12
Egyptian stele with
the name Osiris.

⌐_____⌐3 cm

The influence Egypt extended over Palestine is demonstrated by what may have been the remains of an Egyptian temple from the 13th century, discovered north of the Damascus Gate (Barkay 1990). Fragments of a stone offering table and of the statue of a seated figure were found there as well as two alabaster beakers and a piece of a stone stele with the name Osiris on it (Figure 12). This temple was located along the route to Beth Shean, then an Egyptian garrison city, and may have served Egyptian soldiers.

As mentioned above, a pyramid-like structure was built above the spring

Figure 13   Remains of ancient buildings still visible in the 'City of David' [after Shiloh
(right)   1984, Figure 9].

1/2. Stone and earth filled terraces, 12th   5.   'Burnt house', 7th century BCE.
*   century BCE.*   *6.   Location of the 'house of the bullae',*
3.   Stepped stone structure, 10th century   7th century BCE.
*   BCE.*   *7.   Maccabean tower, 2nd century BCE.*
4.   'House of Ahiel', 7th century BCE.

30

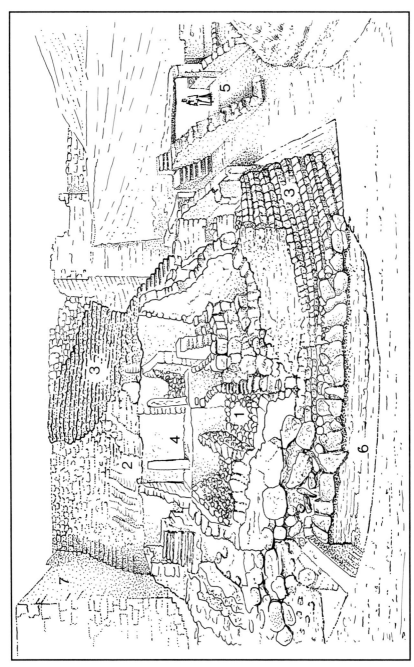

31

Gihon consisting of terraces filled with earth and stones (Figure 13). These terraces climb up the slope, forming horizontal platforms, of which only the largest was suitable for building purposes. The pottery inside the filling of these terraces consisted of forms typical of the beginning of the Iron Age, mixed with some earlier Middle Bronze Age sherds. No later material was found at all, so we can safely date the building of this terrace system in the late 13th or the 12th centuries. The terraces formed the substructure of a large building, probably a fortress, located on a strategic spot dominating the access to the spring. It must have been a tremendous undertaking; the whole system was at least 20 m. high, requiring exquisite building skills. Nothing of the sort has ever been found elsewhere in Palestine; the terraces of Jerusalem stand alone as the major building enterprise dating from the very beginning of the Iron Age. On bedrock underneath the lowest platform a small building from the same period was discovered which had been demolished when the terraces were built.

As nothing has been found of the building on top of the terraces one could argue that it was not a fortress but a temple, or even that no building existed at all and the whole site was an open-air sanctuary. The only argument favouring its interpretation as a fortress is the extreme care that the builders took to choose a strategic location, notwithstanding the large amount of extra work that entailed. They obviously wanted the old Middle Bronze Age city wall on top of the hill, the one with the 'natural moat' described previously, as their northern boundary. However, behind this wall a deep gully had been eroded in bedrock, making it very difficult to build a large complex there. The gully, of which traces have been encountered everywhere in Kenyon's excavations squares, had to be filled in to provide enough building space on top of the hill – hence the terraces. It would have been much easier to locate the building on a spot where no extra work would have been necessary. The fact that they took so much care to fill in the gully just to make it possible to use the old northern fortification line, indicates the defensive (or offensive, if you like) nature of the building.

We do not know who built this system. The pottery shows no 'foreign' influence at all; it is the same repertoire as the local villages display. The architecture, on the other hand, is very sophisticated, although it is difficult to find Egyptian or Phoenician connections. So we only know that at the beginning of the Early Iron Age some people, be it local farmers or more likely strangers, mercenaries serving the Egyptian empire, began to build a fortress on the south-eastern hill of Jerusalem, directly above the spring Gihon.

Since only the substructure for the fortress was found, it is difficult to ascertain the extent of this building complex. We do not know how large the stronghold itself was, how many soldiers it housed, or whether a small village accompanied it on top of the hill. There is also the question of the economic basis of this settlement. It was not a farming community, and no dependent villages ('daughters') have been discovered in the vicinity of this fortress. On the contrary, the settlement of Giloh, a small herdsmen's village that existed some kilometres south of Jerusalem at the beginning of the 12th century, was abandoned quite soon after its foundation, and the other Early Iron Age farming villages were all built at a respectable distance from the fortress. The soldiers may have made a livelihood out of taking tolls from pastoralists who came to water their flocks there; or, more profitably, they may have levied taxes on caravans taking the north-south route over the mountain ridge or the east-west road to Jericho and Transjordan.

The Iron Age

In King David's time (10th century BCE) Jerusalem/Jebus was still a free city-state, however small it may have been. It seems that David wanted to occupy it, not so much because it threatened his growing power, but rather because it was still free, not belonging to any of the clans of Israel or Judah. Since the king wanted to unite the northern and southern tribes into one empire, he needed a capital unconnected with either of the sides. Here he could house his personal army, the Kereti and Peleti, set up his administration, and build a palace and a state temple. In a word – rule as other oriental kings in neighbouring states did. Jerusalem seemed perfect for this goal, because it was located on the boundary line between the northern and the southern tribes, on an important north-south route. Whether David had to capture the city is not exactly clear from the texts. The word *sinnor* ('pipe'/'shaft'?) poses a difficulty; and the obscure references to 'the lame and the blind' are not part of the Chronicles version, and may be later supplements. But occupy it he did, with a very small force and apparently without violence. Nowhere is it stated that the population was massacred or expelled; on the contrary, David seems to have taken over the administration; and Zadok, of apparently Jebusite origin, is listed as one of his two principal priests.

Archaeologically little has been found that can be connected with the few building activities ascribed to David; no trace has remained of the palace he built in the city (2 Sam 5:12) or the wall around it (2 Sam 5:9), nor of his grave in the 'city of David' (1 Kings 2:10). The architectural remains from the 10th century that have been found in Jerusalem are usually assumed to be the work of his son Solomon, who is presented in the Bible as having executed an extensive building programme – presumably to transform the small settlement

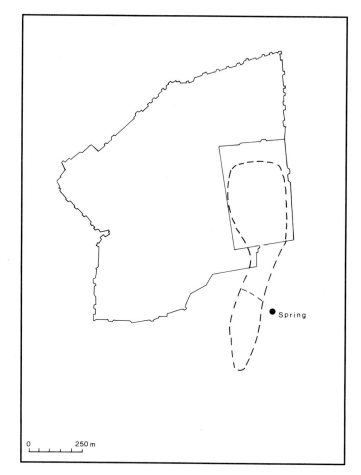

Figure 14
In the 10th century BCE the town expanded to the north where a large terrace was built for temple and palace.

● Spring

0   250 m

of his father into a beautiful 'royal' city, worthy of the mighty king that Solomon was. He is said to have built several palaces and a temple on the Temple Mount, which will be discussed in chapter 3. In doing so he extended the city to almost twice its size (Figure 14). Solomon is also mentioned as the builder of 'the wall of Jerusalem' (1 Kings 9:15) and of a mysterious structure called 'the Millo', a word coming from a Hebrew stem meaning 'to fill'. However, we noted above that the only joint record of this feature in both Samuel-Kings and Chronicles connects it rather with David. Excavations have revealed only a small stretch of a 'casemate wall' on top of the south-eastern hill, which could have formed part of the encircling wall of the new extension of the city.

To the south of this wall more remains from the 10th century were recovered. The terrace system from the 12th century was enlarged on both its eastern and southern sides with a kind of stepped glacis based on heavy stone foundations. Originally the glacis was at least 27 metres high and 40 metres wide at the top, and it would have had a plaster covering. Its function was twofold: to prevent the earlier remains from sliding down the slope, and to form a substructure for an important building on top of it. As the glacis in Jerusalem has a 'filling' of stones, it is one of the candidates for the 'Millo' (compare our discussion in chapter 1). However, as long as no inscription is found stating 'this is the Millo', we can never be sure.

Only a few traces of this building have remained. Part of an interesting incense stand was found nearby (Figure 15), one of the many beautiful objects that must have adorned the rooms. Among the debris found in this area, caused by the destruction of Jerusalem in 587 BCE, was a large 'Proto-Aeolic' capital (Figure 16) and several small ashlars, the quality of material suitable for governmental buildings. The building was located on a strategic point: the north-eastern corner of the old Davidic city, from where the spring Gihon could be protected. Similar stepped stone structures, though much smaller, also dating from the 10th to the 9th centuries, have been discovered at other sites like Lachish, Tell el-Hesi, and Tell en-Nasbeh.

Apart from the above mentioned casemate wall no other town wall from this period has been discovered on the south-eastern hill. The old Middle Bronze Age city wall halfway down the slope was replaced in the 7th century by a new city wall, and there is no evidence at all that the old wall was used or rebuilt in the intervening period. Some remains (small walls, bread ovens) at the foot of the stepped stone glacis testify to scant occupation there, apparently outside the fortifications. The town itself was probably restricted to the top of the hill, defended there by a wall of which no traces have survived the intensive building activities of later periods.

So the casemate wall and the stepped stone structure are the only tangible remains from the 10th century. To get an idea of the city itself we have to look at other sites. In the 10th and 9th centuries BCE, the majority of the population consisted of farmers, living in unwalled villages or small provincial towns. Most cities, however, were not built to house the population, but as 'official cities', founded by the king as centres to control the countryside and to collect taxes. Megiddo (stratum IVA) is a good example of such a 'royal city'. About 75% of the buildings had an official purpose: fortifications, storehouses, barracks and government buildings. No doubt mainly soldiers and officials lived there. But of course Jerusalem had been the ultimate example of such a royal city. It was the city where the king lived and where the main temple was

Figure 15 Pottery stand depicting a bearded man. According to some scholars the figure is carrying an animal; others see him as a captive whose arms are being held by another person [after Shiloh 1984, plate 29:2].

located. A large number of the buildings would have been official buildings and residences for the royal household and the high officials, for the priests, soldiers, clerks, and their servants.

As the wealth of King Solomon depended heavily on long-distance trade, there will have been many warehouses and caravanserais for foreign traders and their convoys. Excavations have revealed that the area between the 'royal compound' in the north and the 'lower city' in the south was still an open space in the 10th century, so maybe the markets were held in that area. It is good to keep in mind that the towns of the 10th century were very small. Jerusalem had grown to encompass about 12 hectares, which was enough to rule the kingdom, but Nineveh in its heyday measured 700 hectares and Babylon 1000 hectares. Even the Palestinian towns of the Middle Bronze Age were much larger; compare Hazor at 84 hectares and Ashkelon at 55 hectares. So while the Jerusalem of King Solomon has become famous for its beautiful

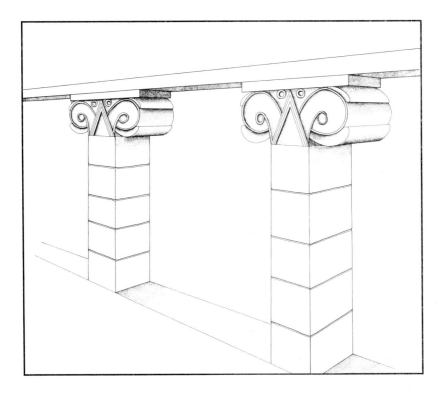

Figure 16   Reconstruction of gate with Proto-Aeolic capitals.

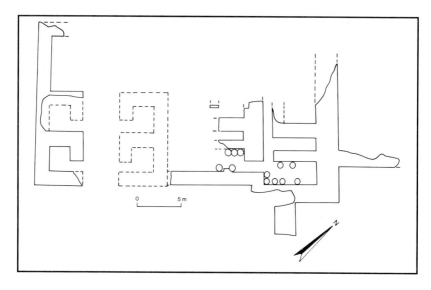

Figure 17   Plan of the Iron Age complex found on the Ophel hill. Left the four-chambered gate, right the 'royal building' where many large storage jars (circles) were discovered [after Mazar & Mazar 1989, plan 26].

temple and even more splendid complex of palaces (to which we have no archaeological access), for the rest it was only a small governmental city.

Estimated population numbers are mostly derived from the area occupied by the city. Modern research tends to reduce the index of population density in ancient towns from the traditional 500 people per hectare to less than 200. If this is correct no more than about 2,000 people would have lived in Jerusalem at that time. In the following centuries the town slowly expanded. In the open area south of the royal quarter more official buildings were erected; excavations have revealed a large tower-like structure dating from the 9th century, possibly a four-chambered gate with an adjoining 'royal building' of which the lower floor was used for storage (Figure 17) (Mazar & Mazar 1989, 50).

On the eastern slope of the south-eastern hill, outside the fortifications, a series of houses was built from the 9th century onwards. This seems to have been a quarter where the common people lived, the small traders and artisans, who settled at the fringe of the town and sold their products to the farmers. These were certainly not rich or important people; the buildings were simple and small, and nothing valuable was found there. Several small caves full of complete pots were discovered behind the houses. When excavated, the first impression was that these were tombs, but there were no human bones inside.

The repertoire of the crockery reminds one rather of the kitchen of an inn: cooking pots, many small jugs and drinking beakers, and only a few storage vessels (Franken & Steiner 1990). Maybe these buildings were some sort of guest-houses, receiving traders doing business in Jerusalem as well as the many pilgrims who visited the city on high festivals. One larger cave also contained dozens of small pottery figurines and some cultic objects. This may have been a small shrine, which will be further discussed in chapter 4.

Traces of occupation from the 9th and 8th centuries have also been found on the western hill, an area not occupied previously. It seems that Jerusalem slowly changed from a governmental town, 'for officials only', to a city where common people lived and worked too. Artisans such as bronze-smiths, bakers, potters and fullers are mentioned in the Bible. There was even a 'street of the bakers' in Jerusalem (Jer 37:21); and it may be that the 'gate of the potsherd' (Jer 19:2) was not an exit for rubbish (compare chapter 1), but led to the potters' district outside the town. New suburbs are mentioned, located outside the City of David: the 'Maktesh', (the mortar) where the merchants lived (Zeph 1:11), and the 'Mishneh', the new or second quarter. This latter was probably a rich, residential part of the town, as the prophetess Huldah and her husband, a high court official, lived there (2 Kings 22:14).

The growth of the population was partly the result of the city's relative wealth and the possibility of making a living there, in a time when the countryside was more and more subject to heavy taxes. The many wars fought (and lost) by the kings of Judah and the heavy tributes they had to pay to the empires of Assyria and Egypt were slowly depleting the resources of the country. Many new inhabitants may also have been refugees from the northern kingdom of Israel, which was attacked and overthrown by the Assyrians in the second half of the 8th century. It is often said that, when Samaria fell in 722 BCE, many Israelites had fled to their southern brothers and sisters.

In 701 BCE the Assyrian king Sennacherib launched a campaign against Judah, an event not only described in the Bible, but also in Assyrian annals found in Nineveh. In the 'Taylor Prism', Sennacherib proudly claims: 'As for Hezekiah, the Judahite, who did not submit to my yoke, 46 of his strong walled cities, as well as the small cities in their neighbourhood, which were without number, [. . .] I besieged and took . . .' (Pritchard 1974, 287-8). Jerusalem is not named among these, and we are told also in the Bible that the city, although besieged, was not taken.

It was the Assyrian threat that induced the kings of Judah to fortify their capital more strongly, according to a repeated theme of the books of Chronicles in the Bible. So King Uzziah (769-741) built 'towers in Jerusalem, at the Gate of the Corner, at the Gate of the Valley, and at the Angle; and he fortified these.' (2 Chron 26:9-10). His son Jotham (741-734) 'carried out considerable work on the wall of Ophel' (2 Chron 27:3). King Hezekiah (715-697) 'strengthened his defences; he had the broken parts of the wall repaired, built towers on it, constructed a second wall on the outer side, strengthened the Millo in the city of David and made quantities of missiles and shields' (2 Chron 32:5). Hezekiah's son Manasseh (697-642) 'rebuilt the outer wall of the Citadel of David, west of Gihon in the wadi, as far as the Fish Gate; it encircled Ophel, and he increased its height very considerably' (2 Chron 33:14).

The geographical indications mentioned here are not very clear; these texts were written by people who lived in Jerusalem and knew exactly where the Gate of the Corner was, or the Angle, while we are left in the dark. When stretches of an Iron Age city wall were discovered on the eastern slope of the south-eastern hill, immediately a discussion broke out among scholars as to which king had built it: was this the wall Hezekiah had constructed, or was it rather the outer wall of the Citadel of David that Manasseh had built? The problem is that archaeological dating can never be precise enough to solve these questions. One should anyway consider the building of a city wall as a lengthy undertaking, started by one king and finished by another; if so, who gets the credit?

Another controversy, outdated now, concerned the size of Jerusalem. The supporters of the 'maximalist' point of view included the western hill in the city from the time of Solomon onwards, based on historical arguments (see Josephus' views above). The 'minimalists' on the other hand (who included Kenyon at first) argued that since no traces of a fortification were discovered there, the Iron Age city did not enclose the western hill, but had been restricted to the south-eastern hill only. This problem was laid to rest once and for all when a seven metres wide city wall was discovered during the excavations in the Jewish Quarter of the Old City. This wall, of which 70 metres could be excavated, encircled part of the western hill, demonstrating that the maximalists were right – but not completely: the wall dated from the end of the 8th century; and this indicates that the incorporation of the western hill occurred in that period, and not before. There is, however, still some discord over how far this wall continued in westerly and especially southerly directions; and thus the exact size of 7th century Jerusalem is still undecided.

Both this wall and the wall on the south-eastern hill were built to protect the undefended quarters that surrounded the old city. Underneath both walls the remains of houses were discovered that had to be abandoned to make room for the new walls, illustrating the words of Isaiah: 'and you pulled down houses to strengthen the wall' (Is 22:10). In the 7th century BCE Jerusalem measured about 50 hectares (in the most maximalistic view) and could have housed up to

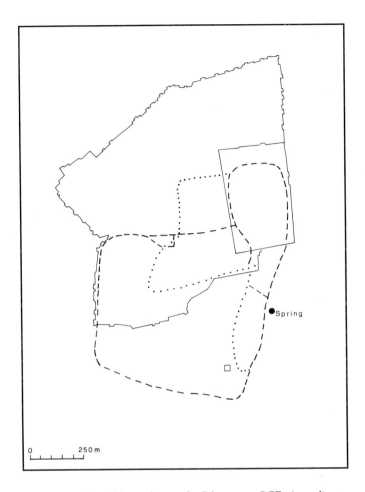

Figure 18   Plan of Jerusalem in the 7th century BCE. According to Avigad the walls extended to the present-day Jaffa Gate in the west. Kenyon imagined a much smaller city, consisting of two separate parts.

10,000 people. This made it by far the largest city of all Palestine. The second in size was Ekron, a flourishing city in the coastal area, which measured 20 hectares, while the size of most other towns ranged from 5-10 ha. Whereas in former days Jerusalem was just one of the many small governmental towns of the kingdom, albeit the most important one, it had now become a real 'metropolis'. As it was also the only town in the region that had escaped destruction

41

or capture by the Assyrians, after a miraculous act of God, this must have made an enormous impression on the people of Judah and their neighbours. And no doubt it also coloured their views of the city and its role in history. Its new strong walls did indeed protect the city for over a hundred years, but of course they also restricted the available breathing and building space (Figure 18). Inside the city it became more and more crowded, so much so that even the stepped stone structure, which had now lost its defensive function, was used as building area. Small terraces were cut into this structure on which some houses were built: the living and working space of several traders, as the finds inside show.

In one house 37 inscribed stone weights were found, together with stone tools such as hammers and anvils. This inventory is typical of the workshop of a bronzesmith, producing and selling small items like jewellery. When the city was destroyed, the smith had apparently succeeded in saving all his valuables and had left only the relatively worthless stone implements. He may have been one of the artisans that were sent to Babylon. In another house 51 'bullae' were discovered, small lumps of unbaked clay used to seal a papyrus document; the sender of the document stamped his or her name into the still soft clay. The house concerned went up in flames in 587 BCE, always a lucky incident for archaeologists. While the documents once attached were destroyed in the fire, the bullae were baked through and through and the names were thus well preserved. The owner of the house was the receiver of the documents, and had kept this correspondence; he may have been a trader doing business with many people, although the excavator thinks it is also possible that the building housed a state archive.

In the south part of the City of David another suburb was discovered. It was dominated by a large building, called the 'Ashlar House' by its excavators, made of big, roughly dressed stones. Compared to the other rather small buildings found, its dimensions were impressive, measuring 12 x 13 metres, and it may have been a public building of some sort. The enormous growth of the city also induced changes in the water supply. The spring Gihon was still the major source of water for the population, but other provisions had been made in the course of time. Most houses had a cistern to catch the unpolluted rain water used for drinking and cooking.

Then there were pools, of which several are mentioned in the Bible, such as the upper pool (2 Kings 18:17), the lower pool (Is 22:9), the King's pool (Neh 2:14) and the old pool (Is 22:11). Several suggestions have been made about their respective locations, but no unanimity has been reached among scholars. Such large rock-cut basins receiving water led by channels in the in the rock were public provisions. This rather dirty water was used mainly for washing clothes, watering the animals, and as irrigation water for the small plots of land on the slopes of the hills around the city. The Bible reports that King Hezekiah 'stopped the upper outlet of the waters of Gihon and directed them down to the west side of the Citadel of David' (2 Chron 32:30) – to provide the population of the large suburb on the western hill with water from the spring Gihon, still the main source of water during the dry season. These waterworks are almost universally identified with the complicated ancient underground system which still brings this water to a pool at the southern end of the city, the pool of Siloam.

The 'Tunnel of Hezekiah' is about 540 m. long and full of bends. Many ingenious solutions have been contrived to explain why the stone cutters did not follow a straight line from the spring to the pool. The most popular solutions were that the bends were a mistake: deep under the ground the workers went in the wrong directions and had to correct their mistakes several times; or the bends were assumed to have been made deliberately to go around some 'holy' site high above, such as the tombs of the kings. The most likely solution, however, is that the workers followed and enlarged a small underground stream bed leading water (and air) from the spring to the south end of the city, a common feature in karstic areas. This would account for its illogical shape, and also explain how the problem of air supply was solved, working so deep underground, as only one air shaft has been discovered (Gill 1991). An inscription was cut into the rock near the exit of the tunnel; it does not confirm the date of the project, but describes the dramatic moment when the gangs of stone cutters, working from two directions, finally met and the water began to flow from Gihon to Siloam.

The inscription was discovered in 1880, and removed from the wall of the tunnel to Istanbul, where it is now housed in the Archaeological Museum. The text of the inscription is set out on six fairly well preserved lines. Arguing, as most do, that it does record the work of Hezekiah's engineers, it is one of the longest pieces of contemporary Hebrew available to us from as early as the end of the 8th century BCE (Figure 19). However, surprisingly for a royal project, the king is not mentioned; and Rogerson and Davies have recently argued (1995) that both tunnel and inscription are from a very much later date.

With the enemy, the Assyrian king Sennacherib, almost before the gates of Jerusalem, King Hezekiah 'and his officers and champions decided to cut off the water supply from the springs situated outside the city. His military staff supported this plan and numbers of people banded together to block all the springs and cut off all the watercourses flowing through the fields. Why, they said, should the kings of Assyria find plenty of water when they arrive?' (2 Chron 32:3-5).

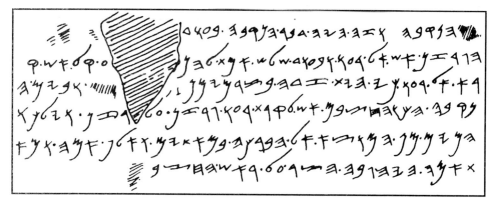

Figure 19 Hezekiah's tunnel inscription: '. . . the tunnelling. And this was the description of the tunnelling. While . . . the axe, each one towards his fellow, and while there were still three cubits to . . . hear[d] one calling to his fellow, for there was a 'crack' in the rock on the right and [on the lef]t (or 'from the south [to the nor]th'). And at the end of the tunnelling the diggers hacked each one to meet his fellow, axe upon axe. And there came the waters from the source to the pool for two hundre[d and] a thousand cubits. And a hund[dr]ed cubits was the height of the rock above the head of the digger . . .

This verse refers most likely to a third underground system connected with Gihon: the Siloam Channel. This is a tunnel cut along the edge of the slope, with outlets or windows in the rock (the 'springs') allowing the water to irrigate the farmed terraces on the slope below (the 'watercourses flowing through the fields'). This system fed what is now called Birket el Hamra, a large pool at the south end of the south-eastern hill, outside the fortifications. No wonder the officials decided to stop the outlets to deny the approaching enemy any water. This system was never used again; recent excavations revealed that the outlets were still closed with large stones. The Assyrian pressure could be relieved at the expense of paying a heavy tribute. A hundred years later, however, the Babylonian king Nebuchadnezzar succeeded where the Assyrians had failed. First he took the city in 597 BCE but did not destroy it, as is described in the Bible and in Babylonian annals. He appointed a new king and took many inhabitants as captives to Babylon. Then when this King Zedekiah rebelled, he came again and laid siege to the city for eleven months.

As expected, 'famine was raging in the city' (2 Kings 25:3), which has now been confirmed by a surprising source. In one of the houses a stone toilet seat was found connected with a plastered latrine pit, the content of which was analysed. It seems that in the last days of the siege the inhabitants of Jerusalem lived on a meagre diet of salad plants, herbs and spices. The principal foods of the common people, wheat, barley, lentils and peas, were noticeably absent, while intestinal parasites such as whipworm and tapeworm formed a real plague (Cahill 1991).

After Nebuchadnezzar had taken the city in 587 BCE, he 'burnt down all the houses', and 'demolished the walls surrounding Jerusalem' (2 Kings 25:10-11). Traces of this destruction have been encountered all over the city. The houses on the south-eastern hill were all destroyed by a fierce fire, which had brought down the upper floors and filled the rooms with rubble. The city wall there was taken down by the Babylonians, and a mass of stones and rubble covered the slope of the hill, leaving it uninhabitable for centuries. On the western hill, outside a tower connected with the city wall there, the most dramatic witness of the fight for the city was discovered: the surface at the foot of the tower was covered with charred wood, ashes and soot in which several iron and bronze arrowheads from both defenders and attackers were found, testifying to the bitter struggle that had taken place there. The palace complex and Solomon's beautiful temple were destroyed completely, a tragedy over which the exiles deeply mourned 'by the rivers of Babylon' (Ps 137). Notwithstanding the many thousands that had been led away in exile, the country was not completely abandoned. The Babylonians had left 'some of the humbler country people as vineyard workers and ploughmen' (2 Kings 25:12), and Gedaliah was appointed governor of Judah. However, he had his seat not in Jerusalem, but in Mizpah, not far away.

The Persian and Hellenistic Periods

There is some archaeological evidence for a continuation of occupation. At Ketef Hinnom, by the Scots Kirk in modern Jerusalem, some rock-cut tombs have been found, which had continued in use from the Iron Age through the Babylonian until the Persian period (Barkay 1986). Exceptionally one tomb had never been discovered by grave robbers, and it testifies to the prosperity of the people who continued to live in or near the city; gold and silver jewellery, cosmetic palettes, bronze kohl sticks and faience ornaments were amongst the finds. Of course these were the graves of the rich and mighty, maybe officials or traders, who for some reason wanted to be buried a little further from the temple mount, and in the vicinity of the main north-south road.

After the Persian empire had broken the power of the Babylonians the Bible reports how King Cyrus issued an edict in 538 BCE giving the Jews permission to return to their homeland and to rebuild their temple (Ezra 1:2-4). The first group of exiles, headed by Sheshbazzar, 'prince of Judah', are

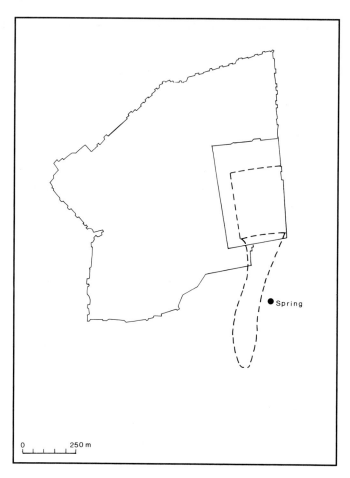

Spring

0   250 m

*Figure 20 In the Persian and Early Hellenistic periods the city was
restricted to the south-eastern hill and the temple mount.*

said to have taken with them the temple treasury, consisting of the thousands
of gold and silver vessels that Nebuchadnezzar had pillaged. Then, in 520
BCE, Zerubbabel started to rebuild the temple of Jerusalem, a laborious
undertaking that was finished only in 515 BCE. This temple was probably a
simple building, '60 cubits high and 60 cubits in width' (Ezra 6:3), about 30 x
30 m. It stood on the terrace that Solomon had built for his temple.

The city itself, however, was still in ruins. The population was very small
and no houses had yet been built when Nehemiah was sent as governor to

Figure 21   Impression on pottery of a seal with the letters YHWD, *the Persian District Judah.*

Jerusalem by King Artaxerxes; we do not know exactly which Artaxerxes this was, so the date of this journey is still being debated, but it was probably in 445 BCE. An Aramaic inscription on papyrus, found at Elephantine on the Nile, and dated to 408 BCE, mentions Bagohi as the current governor (Cowley 1923). Nehemiah had permission and ample funds to start re-building the city. In Jerusalem he made his famous tour around the city, going secretly by night around the ruined walls and burned gates to inspect the damage (Neh 2:11-16). It is a well-told story. In the exceptionally short time of 52 days the city walls were re-erected; every family or professional group had been assigned a part of the walls or a gate to restore. When the project was finished, the walls were dedi-cated with a glorious tour by the officials and priests over the top of the walls (Neh 12:27-43). We used this text in Chapter 1 to locate the gates and to calcu-late the size of the city of Nehemiah (Figure 20). But we have to admit that no consensus has been reached and a maximalist-against-minimalist struggle has been taken up over this issue too.

Recent excavations on the western hill have found no Persian remains there at all, demonstrating that the city was limited to the south-eastern hill, in that period just as in the times of King David. In view of the small population, and the location of the water supply, this should come as no surprise. At the top of the south-eastern hill foundations of a tower and part of the city wall from the Persian period were excavated, while the slope of this hill was covered with debris in which many stamped jar handles were found, bearing the name *yhd* or *yhwd*: *Yehud*, the Persian name for the district Judah (Figure 21).

In 333 BCE Alexander the Great occupied the city and after his death it fell to the sovereignty of the Egyptian Ptolemies. The town was still very small, but it seems that over time the temple gained more importance, and some commentators even speak of a 'temple state', in which the priesthood was dominant, although they had no real political power. Hardly any archaeological finds have been discovered from this period besides some Ptolemaic coins, while stamped jar handles attest to the import of wine from Rhodes. It was only in the period after 220 BCE that Jerusalem slowly expanded under the Seleucids till it resumed its former glory in the days of Herod the Great.

3

Temple and King's House

The Site

It is as we turn to explore Jerusalem's most important buildings that our reading of the biblical texts has to bear much more of the strain. However, careful observation provides some control. We have reason to believe that both complexes – or at least the Temple – were in that part of ancient Jerusalem which archaeology has been unable to penetrate – somewhere within or on that sacred area which, typical of Jerusalem and its divisions, is called different names in different languages and religions: the Arabic and Muslim *al-Ḥaram al-Sharif* or 'Noble Sanctuary' and Hebrew and Jewish *Har ha-Bayit* or 'Mount of the House' (commonly 'Temple Mount'). Since the beginnings of modern investigation in the mid-nineteenth century, religious and political susceptibilities have precluded anything more than superficial examination by archaeologists of any part of the site.

The entire walled and gated sacred enclosure which contains within it two of Islam's most prominent shrines, the Dome of the Rock near its centre and the Mosque of *al Aqsa* at the southern end, is a man-made platform. And the man who had most of the present platform made was Herod the Great, perhaps the most successfully ambitious building patron Jerusalem and a hundred kilometres around have ever seen. That platform, itself a prestigious achievement, is nothing other than a grandiose set of foundations for his rebuilding of the Jewish Temple in Jerusalem (Figure 22). The Temple itself and its immediate precincts were destroyed by the Roman general (and later Emperor) Titus some hundred years after Herod's thirty year rebuilding work began. Herod's monumental foundations had to wait a further six hundred years before they were again fitly crowned by the still 'noble' shrines erected in Islam's first century. And it is possible that it was finally in this early Islamic period that the platform itself was extended a little to the north, so achieving its present extent. Even today, when most cities are much more spacious than in ancient times, the large open area of this sacred enclosure impresses the visitor, whether from within or with the 'grandstand' view from the greater

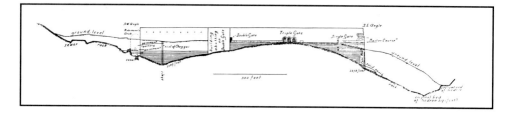

Figure 22 Section through Jerusalem showing the Kidron valley and the al-Ḥaram al Sharif *(temple mount) with the mosques. This terrace was erected by Herod the Great in the 1st century BCE for his temple. It was built over a small valley called 'Cheesemaker's Valley', which is not visible any more. Both valleys have been filled in with rubble.*

heights of the Mount of Olives or Mount Scopus. And still today, the height of its walls is impressive from these same vantage points on the eastern hills.

Josephus reports that Herod doubled the size of the previous temple area. One large joint is clearly open to view: on the east wall of the *Haram*, just over thirty metres north from its south-east corner, Herodian masonry to the south is laid against an earlier wall to the north. When we recognise this, we have located both the eastern and the southern precinct walls before Herod. His 'doubling' of the former area did not involve any further encroachment on the valley to the east: it was achieved by the extension southwards of some thirty metres just mentioned, an extension westwards (encroaching on the valley that gives its name to 'Valley Street' (*al-Wad*) in the present 'Old City') and possibly northwards too. It is certainly from the south, where the natural slope is steepest and where later accumulations of debris have now been removed, that the vastness of Herod's enterprise makes its greatest impact.

Not only was the extent of his work on the sacred site huge. Also, unlike most builders till recent times, he did not build on top of the foundations or rubble of his predecessors – so preserving some of them for our excavation and inspection – but cleared the area to bedrock and built directly on that. These facts have persuaded many archaeologists, who have also studied his building techniques at other sites, that they would find little if anything belonging to earlier periods underneath the Jerusalem platform even if they were permitted to explore freely and excavate. If they mean 'under his own new extensions to the Temple platform', that may be good judgement. Yet how much did he reconstruct of the old platform of the former Temple building? Without excavation in Jerusalem, we cannot know. However, archaeology elsewhere in the country may offer some useful clues. Some decades after the division of Solomon's kingdom on his death, the city of Samaria was constructed as capital of northern Israel. It was also constructed on a steep hill; and its acropolis was built on top of a huge level rectangular artificial platform of some 1.6 hectares (about 4 acres). Its length and breadth were each some two-fifths of the dimensions of the present *Haram*. But whether Samaria fell short of or outdid Solomon's Jerusalem of the previous century we cannot tell. In a similar period to Samaria, southern Judah's second city, Lachish, had a royal building atop a large built-up base.

Herod's builders and their more modest predecessors widened quite a narrow natural north-south ridge by extending it into or over the valleys to east and west; and they raised the ground level of this widened area to within a few metres of the natural summit of that ridge. Of all the natural narrow rocky ridge, only tiny portions at the very top are now exposed to view. Of these, the best-known is right underneath the 'dome' over the 'rock'; another is accessible under a *qubbah* at the north-west corner of the esplanade. We know that the natural rock slopes more gently eastwards from this summit than westwards; and that fact influences our discussion of the precise location of the temple. Most scholars suppose that Herod's temple itself, or at least one of its central elements, was the previous occupant of the site of the Dome of the Rock. Most assume that Herod's temple had occupied the site of its Judaean predecessors. But, perhaps because we have so little rock to examine, we also have no 'hard evidence' – and reasoning or speculation take over. Not all scholars take this view. Some locate it further south, thinking that the 'rock' at 500m distance is too far from the likely northern extremity of David's city. Others place it still further north, in alignment with the Golden Gate. The present Golden Gate was constructed in the early Islamic period – and we know that just outside it there is evidence of an earlier gate, though it is not known just how much earlier. It is supposed that the present gate, imbued as it is with legend and expectation, or its prececessor was the spot through which the rising sun had illumined the Temple on a key date in the year. Biblical Yahweh is often spoken of in language used elsewhere of the sun-god – Psalm 104 has close associations with an Egyptian Hymn to Aten, the Sun-disc. In this connection, we should note the mutilated poetic lines in Solomon's prayer at the dedication of the Temple. They can be restored as follows from the Greek Bible:

Sun has he set in the heavens,
But Yahweh has intended to dwell in deep darkness.
Surely I have built a lordly house for you,
A place for you to dwell in for ever. (1 Kings 8:12-13)

However, 'sun' is a feminine noun in Hebrew and its closest ancient Semitic relatives. And that suggests to some scholars that it was as a symbol of his consort that Sun was associated with Yahweh. The lines certainly insist on the subordination of the sun to Yahweh: he himself chooses to live in the deep darkness of the most holy place within the Temple. The solar alignment of the shrine may have allowed her to come to him on certain sacred days. We should remember in this context that the Feasts of Passover and of Tabernacles (*Succoth*) are close to the Spring and Autumn equinoxes.

If the rock at the centre of the present octagonal building was also one of the focal points of the earlier Jerusalem shrines, including Solomon's, then presumably that natural summit was either underneath the most holy place within the Temple, at its inner (western) end, or it was the spot outside that building, opposite the east door, where the great altar of sacrifice was.

(a) Tradition suggests one answer. It associates the rock with the site upon a divinely indicated mountain at which Abraham was prepared to sacrifice his only son to God (Gen 22; 2 Chron 3:1). Where more appropriate to suppose that the continuing great altar for sacrifice was sited? Yet need we assume that the 'top' of a mountain implies its very peak, rather than just somewhere close to it?

(b) The lie of the land suggests the other answer. The floor level of the cubic 'Holy of Holies' was probably higher than in the main hall of the temple. And so, from the building engineering point of view, it would have been easier to site that raised innermost end of the building on the summit with the main hall to its east where the natural slope is gentler – but much harder to start from the exterior great altar on the summit, and construct the whole temple to the west of it where the natural rock descends much more quickly. In addition, such a reconstruction would place the 'holy of holies' much closer to the present (apparently Herodian) western wall. If that is the right answer, then the location of the open-air altar of sacrifice opposite its east door may be marked today by the Dome of the Chain which stands almost precisely at the centre of the huge sacred enclosure. Its function is a puzzle: it has been thought (improbably) to be a model for the great Dome of the Rock beside it, or (more probably) either a treasury or the marker of the navel of the earth, or conceivably both. But it may also preserve the known location of an earlier vital element of the same holy site.

So much by way of deduction from our observations in Jerusalem's sacred precinct. What of the biblical writings – are they to be treated as primary evidence?

The Biblical Evidence

The Books of Samuel-Kings and Chronicles were first written, and several times rewritten, in a period which only began after Jerusalem's capture and deportation by Babylon. As we noted in the introductory chapter, the starting point for this literary history is easily defined if we recognise that these two biblical collections share a common source which ended with a report of the story of Jerusalem's fall. That fact in itself sets the minimum distance between David and Solomon and the writing of the common source at four hundred years. The successor histories which we now read in the Bible are all the more distant. We know that Josephus, later still, was seriously misinformed about the location of Zion and David's tomb. That is hardly surprising in a city which had changed shape several times – expanded, contracted, expanded again – in the thousand years that separated him from David.

How reliable then is the Bible's information about the Jerusalem of David and Solomon? Its writers were somewhat closer to the events than Josephus; they knew a sacred area which had not yet been transformed by Herod's masons. However, they were on the same side as Josephus of the gulf caused by the cataclysm of the Babylonian conquest, which had brought to an end the world of David's line and of the royal and many of the religious institutions they shaped.

The reports in these books of Solomon's building works in Jerusalem offer a typical illustration of the interrelationships of the books as a whole. The most detailed report is in the traditional Hebrew text of the book of Kings: as the basis of most modern translations of the Bible, it is also the most familiar one to the majority of readers. The ancient Greek version of Kings offers a less detailed report; and the Book of Chronicles a much shorter one still. Most commentators suppose that each of these others is an abridgement, less or more radical, of the original Hebrew text in Kings. And many claim that this 'original' was itself based on a much older document or documents preserved in the archives of the temple/palace complex. However, we should make our approach on another tack. We have to recognise that ancient scholarly scribes were more accustomed to adding material to the texts they were copying (either to make something clearer, or simply because more information had come to their hand) than deleting some of the contents (except when their eye jumped by mistake). We should start instead from the material common to the Hebrew and Greek versions of Kings and to Chronicles, the material which each in turn has expanded. When we do so, our reservoir of primary source-material is very much reduced:

(a) Kings and Chronicles do agree almost entirely over the various cultic implements associated with the temple: molten sea; ten lavers; pots, shovels, and basins; lampstands, lamps, tongs, dishes for incense; and many other tools (1 Kings 7:23-50; 2 Chron 4:2-22).

(b) As to the Temple structure itself, the text common to our three versions is very sketchy: all agree that Solomon began building the temple in the second month of the fourth year of his reign; that the house of Yahweh was some 27 metres long (60 cubits); that the vestibule in front of the nave was 9 metres, opposite the width of the house, by 4.5 metres (deep); and that he overlaid the house with gold; that two winged cherubim, with a wing-length of 2.25 metres, occupied the innermost most holy place; and that tall pillars named Jachin and Boaz were set up outside the vestibule of the Temple.

(c) The common and primary source had offered no systematic account of the King's House as a building project of Solomon. It simply said in summary fashion that he did build the King's House (1 Kings 9:1,10; 2 Chron 7:11; 8:1); and it mentioned here and there within the Solomon story individual royal apartments, both ceremonial and residential (1 Kings 10:17-21; 2 Chron 9:16-20).

Many scholars who might be prepared to give at least some credence to this main thesis will still wish to claim that the royal palace represents the exception which proves the rule. They will maintain that the principal components of the non-religious buildings of state had indeed been listed in the source – it 'must have been' to such a listing that the summary mention retained by the Chronicler referred. And they will explain that the Chronicler, writing long after the collapse of the monarchy and independent government, knew no royal palace in his own Jerusalem. He therefore omitted from his source details of such earlier structures as were, unlike the Temple, of no continuing relevance to his people.

And yet the palace need not be the exception that 'proves the rule'. Auld's thesis can be vigorously defended here too. It may well be that the post-exilic common source did describe only the Temple and offered no details about the palace of earlier times precisely because, in the community where it was written, such apartments had no further relevance. The concluding summary in that source simply notes that it took the suitably round figure of twenty years to complete Solomon's work on 'the house of Yahweh and the house of the king'. It gave no details; but it did acknowledge that such a building had been built by Solomon. The Book of Kings is much more hostile to Solomon than either the common source or the Book of Chronicles. It practises some ironic knife-twisting in the body of the developing Solomon-legend; a classic case is its additions at the beginning and end of the Solomon story: 'Solomon loved Yahweh (1 Kings 3:3) . . . and many foreign women (1 Kings 11:1)'. It repeatedly 'clarifies' the legend by means of telling juxtapositions. And it is typical of this sort of editorial character assassination that, within its section on Solomon the builder, it develops its polemic against the king by building a report of his palace-construction (1 Kings 7:1-12) out of scattered references elsewhere to throne-room and judgement hall (1 Kings 10:17-21) – and dividing the twenty-year building period mentioned in its source into components of seven for the Temple and thirteen (roughly twice as many) for his own palace.

Polite or pious respect for ancient religious texts might have predisposed us to find in the Bible a good deal of neutrally preserved archaic information. However, once we start reading Kings, and Chronicles too, as contentious, tendentious documents of religious politics, we have to reckon with a more heady mix. Kings, to take one example, says that the Holy of Holies was separated from the main hall of the Temple by wooden doors – Chronicles, by a heavy curtain. Most commentators take Kings at face value, and suppose that Chronicles has adjusted the facts to accommodate them to the tradition of the tent shrine of the desert wandering period, which had a curtain at the same position. Possibly so. But equally possibly we may be dealing with rival views of how the reconstructed temple should be fitted out. Ezekiel 40-48 also contains useful historical information about the Temple amidst many dreams and claims for a future reconstruction that were not realised. We expect this of prophecy. But in Kings and Chronicles too we find a similar mix in what appears to be straightforward narrative about the past. The eye of the 'historian' is often focused quite as much on issues of present and future as on the past and what happened then. It is with a great deal of caution therefore that we must view some of the classic attempts, based mostly on Kings, to reconstruct the plans of Solomon's temple-palace complex.

Illustration

Granted that excavation at the site itself has not been possible, and that in any case it might not produce many results, our next move must be to see if we can correlate the source we have reconstructed which lies behind the biblical books of Kings and Chronicles with our general archaeological knowledge of temple buildings and their paraphernalia in the ancient Levant. Several useful parallels are regularly quoted:

(a) for the three-element structure of the temple building (entrance portico, main hall, and innermost holy place), the Late Bronze Age temple at Hazor in northern Israel and the temple at *tell ta'yinat* in Syria – and that parallel commends itself to many researchers, because the temple there forms part of a larger palace complex which is used in turn to clarify the much sparser details provided in the Bible about the Jerusalem palace (Figure 23);

(b) for the two huge bronze columns (nine metres in height, and two

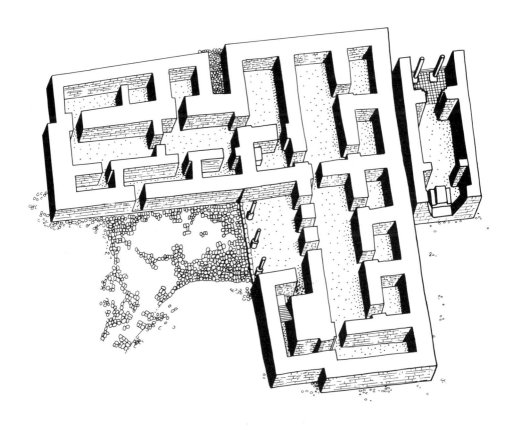

Figure 23   Isometric drawing of the palace of tell ta'yinat in Turkey. Adjoining the palace is a small three-part temple with two pillars. Both buildings date from the 8th century BCE.

in diameter), named Jachin and Boaz, within or just in front of the entrance portico, the same temple at Hazor, and the 10th century temple at Arad in southern Judah, and also the columns similarly placed before a model of a shrine preserved in Beirut, and held to represent a temple to Melqart of Tyre;

(c) for the raised cella (or innermost holy sanctuary) and also the large altar in front of the temple, again the temple at Arad;

(d) for the molten sea of bronze, a large basin from Cyprus (now in the Louvre, Paris), also decorated with bull figures, carved from soft limestone – but only just over two metres in diameter, as compared with some five metres (10 cubits) in the case of the sea cast for Jerusalem;

(e) for the bronze lavers on their stands, again there are comparable examples from Cyprus, but much smaller (Figure 24);

(f) for the many lamps, cups, fire-pans, incense burners, and the like, numerous illustrative examples.

Yet we have to admit that what the Bible describes is more magnificent than we can fully illustrate from elsewhere. The bronze columns, the 'sea', and the mobile lavers are much larger than our Cypriot comparators. Nothing of what the Bible describes has survived for our inspection: indeed its own report of the Babylonian sack of Jerusalem specifically mentions the break-up and removal of all the large metal objects. Yet what the Bible reports about these molten accoutrements of the Temple is less amazing than its accounts of Solomon's gold income from trade and gifts; and these latter reports have recently been vigorously if not entirely convincingly defended (Millard 1989).

The Bible says that Solomon's metal-working was done in the Jordan valley in the area of Succoth. Given the winds there, that is inherently probable; and large ovens of the Early Iron Age were found at Deir Alla on the east side of the middle Jordan valley. Deir Alla is identified by many scholars as, or as near to, the site of ancient Succoth. The excavator, Henk Franken, interpreted them as bronze ovens, although they are much larger than any bronze oven known from that or earlier periods (Franken 1969). What is remarkable is that casting a roughly hemispherical 'sea' with a diameter of five metres does represent a prodigious feat of metal-working – not to speak of transporting its great weight up the mountains to Jerusalem. And indeed the molten 'sea' has so much caught the imagination of scholars that it often figures in academic courses on art history or the history of technology. It may all have been exaggerated in memory. Yet equally, the greater the amounts and the impressiveness of the metal involved, the more likely it was to have been plundered and, as we might say today, 'recycled' for an invader's capital city.

*Figure 24   Bronze laver found in Larnaca, Cyprus. Such lavers may
have been used in the temple.*

It should, therefore, perhaps not surprise us that only more modest comparators have survived for modern inspection.

The information in Kings about the 'king's house(s)' is so sparse and uncoordinated that even scholars who view it as authentic primary information differ about whether one building (or cluster of buildings) is implied, or whether quite separate structures are envisaged. It is often said that the information could be a non-specialist's description of a *bit ḥilani*: a type of royal building quite widely known from the ancient Levant. *bit ḥilani* is an Akkadian term which refers to a palace with a colonnaded entrance porch. Although the word *ḥilani* looks similar to *ḥalon*, the Hebrew word for 'window', this connection is apparently quite fortuitous. It is equally true that many other reconstructions are possible. It is worth emphasising again that the most detailed biblical information available to us is the notes in 1 Kings 7:1-12; and that these may have been compiled only some time after the destruction of the buildings in question, and in a period when there was no longer a king in Jerusalem.

In one important respect the comparators we have listed for the shape of

Solomon's Temple and the nature of many of the associated objects – parallels from Lebanon, Syria, and Cyprus – do point in the same direction as one basic element of the biblical tradition: that Solomon, and indeed David too, had a close relationship with Hiram from Tyre. The reports of this relationship had two main aspects. They traded in partnership with each other on a large scale. And Solomon leant heavily for constructional help on this Hiram, who had supplied craftsmen, labourers, and materials for his work in Jerusalem.

How these links should be evaluated in terms of religious influence is another matter. The traditional view, deduced straightforwardly from the pages of the Bible (though not stated there in so many words), is that David and Solomon fatefully imported the alien values of the ancient Levant into an earlier and purer form of Israel's culture and religion. However, at our critical distance, it is possible to appreciate just how indebted to the centuries of royalty the whole biblical tradition really was. The High Priest of the Second Temple period had several of the trappings and responsibilities of the earlier kings. After the collapse the nation itself became styled the 'servant' and 'chosen one' of its God Yahweh – titles which had earlier been used to designate the king. Such terminology, which we can see being freshly reminted in the exilic period in the central chapters of the Book of Isaiah (40-55), is also important in the book of Deuteronomy. Written in a similar period, it applies this fresh language to its account of Israel's early beginnings and teaches of a nation 'chosen' by Yahweh in ancient times. Greater interest in the nation and its servant role and chosenness alongside Yahweh's chosen servant the king is also typical of some of the expansions that have turned Judah's older story about her kings into the present Book of Kings. The Books of Kings and Deuteronomy share a cautious approach to the institution of kingship. These later ideas, this developed language, which emerged after Jerusalem's exile to Babylon, had a profound effect on the way the nation's most ancient traditions were shaped and reshaped in this same period. The resulting dominant view emerged that Israel's first great leaders were not kings – that kingship and all that it entailed was an alien implant. But it is more likely that the non-royal and even anti-royal flavour of the Bible's traditions about the period before David and Solomon was directly influenced by hostility to Judah's kings in the period after their collapse.

Temple and Treasury

'Temple' conveys to most modern readers the idea of a prominent building for religious purposes. And, although Temple is a rather free rendering of the expressions used in the Hebrew Bible for the building in question, we would have similar expectations of a structure called 'the House of Yahweh' or 'God's House' and containing in its innermost recesses a cube-shaped chamber where the deity was held to 'live' or 'sit enthroned' amidst deepest darkness. But our assumptions are neither completely wide of the mark nor yet quite appropriate. We need to remember that the 'house' was only part of the total installation; and that other important elements such as the great 'Sea' and the altar of sacrifice were outside it. That means that many important religious actions happened outside, or in the vicinity of, the 'temple' – and not inside that 'house'. And we need to remember that the biblical story of Judah's kings also portrays 'Yahweh's house' as what we would call a treasury rather than a shrine. The first mention in that story of metal objects related to the 'house' concerns ritual pots and snuffers and the bronze pillars and 'sea' (1 Kings 7:15-50) which were prepared before the temple's consecration. However, the many subsequent reports of moving metal objects into and out of this building (and often the 'king's house' as well) have to do with what we would call monetary rather than sacral transactions. No wonder that the goldsmiths had a particular interest in Nehemiah's repair of the city wall on either side of the Watch Gate which gave directly into the Temple – their workrooms had been just inside.

These two neighbouring 'houses' then functioned as the state treasury. Some of the deposits in the temple had been involuntary taxes. Some were voluntary 'dedications' to the deity which could be 'redeemed' at a set percentage – what we would term safe deposits, for which a charge was made. 1 Kings 7:51 reports that, as soon as the building was complete and before it was consecrated, Solomon deposited in the treasuries of the 'house of Yahweh' the 'holy things' or 'dedications' of David his father. It was these deposits that were forcibly looted by Shishak of Egypt, or Jehoash of Israel, or Nebuchadnezzar of Babylon; and hardly more voluntarily despatched by Asa to buy Syrian help against Baasha of Israel, or by Hezekiah to buy off Sennacherib of Assyria. The Book of Chronicles reports quite summarily the Chaldean destruction of Jerusalem:

> And all the vessels of the house of God, great and small, and the treasures
> of the house of Yahweh, and the treasures of the king and of his princes,
> all these he brought to Babylon. And they burned the house of God,
> and broke down the wall of Jerusalem, and burned all its palaces
> with fire, and destroyed all its precious vessels. (2 Chron 36:18-19)

The Books of Kings and of Jeremiah report the sack of the city at greater length. And, although they make no mention of the destruction of sacred or royal 'treasures', they do repeat the inventory of 1 Kings 7:15-50 and report its removal to Babylon – some objects whole and some in pieces (2 Kings 25:13-17; Jer 52:17-23). This expanded report carries the suggestion that the key objects of the nation's religion were in exile along with its key people. And in Kings this listing of the metal implements for the temple at both beginning and end of the book functions like a bracket round all the other more monetary talk of temple and palace treasures.

Another Palace?

Much of this chapter has involved close examination of the biblical evidence for sacred and royal buildings on a site that is unavailable for direct archaeological examination. However, the discussion should not end without mention of a building complex in the vicinity of Jerusalem which appears to have left little if any trace in the Bible. The site in question is called Rachel's Hill (*ramat raḥel* in Hebrew); is roughly midway between the 'Old City' of Jerusalem and Bethlehem; and, from a height similar to the Mount of Olives, has a fine view of both towns. The excavations led by Y. Aharoni in 1954-62 showed that it had been first settled in the ninth to eighth centuries BCE, with a royal citadel surrounded by gardens and farms. The late seventh century saw a substantial expansion to a palace of some 75m x 50m within an artificially levelled enclosure eight times that size. This had been built for one of Judah's last kings; and destroyed very soon after with Jerusalem early in the sixth century BCE. The scale, though somewhat more modest, and some of the building features and decoration are reminiscent of the royal enclosure at Samaria – and help to justify using Samaria to imagine what 'may have been' in Jerusalem itself. Fragments of Proto-Aeolic capitals and a window balustrade demonstrate the quality of this sizeable residence. The excavator supposed that this was the palace for whose luxury Jeremiah 22:13-19 condemns King Jehoiakim; and identified it with Beth-hakkerem ('Vineyard House') of Jeremiah 6:1 and Nehemiah 3:14 (Aharoni 1979: 351, 395). That place in turn is regularly identified with the 'Karem', listed in the verse missing from Hebrew (and most English) Bibles after Joshua 15:59, but preserved in the ancient Greek translation. Kallai (1986: 393) mentions some difficulties about this identification. In any case, since the border between Judah and Jerusalem ran so close to the south-east tip of built-up Jerusalem, this palace must have been situated in what Joshua 15 envisaged as a district south of Jerusalem, and not part of that city. A rebuilt citadel was functioning again there in the fourth century BCE.

The Temple Rebuilt

The so-called 'Second Temple' is the temple reconstructed after the Babylonians themselves had fallen in turn to the Persians. Like its predecessor it functioned as both shrine and bank; and in that period there was no adjoining king's house with its own treasury. Though no longer under the patronage of a king, it was no less significant politically. Indeed many scholars today portray Jerusalem of the period, with the reduced territory of Judah round about, as a 'civic-temple community' of a sort found frequently under Persian Achaemenid rule: in this view city and surrounding lands were more or less an appendage of the temple. There is a widespread 'sense' that the second temple was less glorious than the first, but little hard evidence. On the one side, it is hard to interpret with certainty the note in Ezra 3:12 about the mixture of weeping and pleasure among those witnesses of the laying of the new foundations who had known the former building. On the other, our reports of the Solomonic building may well be exaggerated recollections of a golden age. Then again, though texts from the Persian period talk more than earlier biblical texts about the house of God as a 'house of prayer', other texts seem to understand the whole of Jerusalem as that 'house', and not just its temple.

Finally, remembering how long some traditions persist in Jerusalem, we recall again as we noted at the beginning of this chapter one of the explanations for the much smaller Dome of the Chain which stands to the east of the great Dome of the Rock: that it functioned as a treasury. Even though it lacked walls, its contents were protected by the sanctity of the site. This identification is helped by the similar, and almost contemporary, treasury in the courtyard of the Great Mosque of Damascus.

4

Life and Death
in Ancient Jerusalem

After we have discussed life and death there will not be much left to talk about, religion included! The ancient Jerusalemite would not have readily discussed what we call religious matters separately from 'life and death'. Yet, since many of our modern readers have different expectations, we have contrived a space for 'religion' in the midst of living and dying.

Life . . .

In the 7th century and the beginning of the 6th, the last period before the destruction of the city by the Babylonians in 587 BCE, Jerusalem was a thriving city. The threat of the Assyrians had forced the kings of Judah to improve the defences of their capital Jerusalem; and so the new suburbs that had spread around the City of David were surrounded by heavy city walls. These walls, of which some portions still survive, 'fixed' the circumference of the city, thus allowing us to calculate the size of the town and the number of its inhabitants: in the 7th century BCE Jerusalem measured about 50 hectares and housed up to 10,000 people.

The new city quarters were mainly inhabited by rich merchants and artisans with their families and servants, while the royal court, the high officials and the temple servants had their dwellings on the Temple Mount and the Ophel hill just south of it. The poorer part of the population may have lived outside the city walls. The inhabitants had very likely been segregated spatially according to their profession and status and maybe also to their origin. We know from 1 Kings 20:34 that merchants from Damascus were living in Samaria and vice versa. Likewise Jerusalem will have housed traders from other countries, and presumably in their own quarters. Several inscriptions have been found bearing South Arabian names written in South Arabian script but scratched onto local jugs; and that evidence may signify Arab traders living in the city (Shiloh 1985).

A large part of Jerusalem's wealth came from trade with neighbouring regions. Items of local produce, such as wine, olive oil, perfumes, dates and

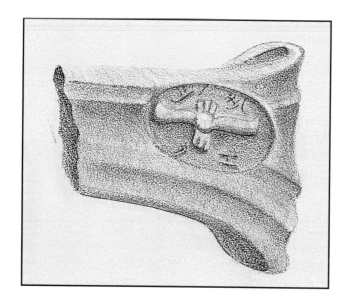

Figure 25
Impression of a
LMLK-*seal in the*
handle of a jar.
Depicted are a two-
winged scarab (?)
and the consonants
of the word
la-melek
('belonging to the
king').

figs, were in high demand elsewhere. Grain must also have been important: in Nineveh a document has been found recording a sale of wheat, transacted in the city by two Babylonian merchants, which was measured 'according to the Judahite *sutu*' (a grain measure which appears in Hebrew as *se'ah*), presumably because the grain came from Judah packed according to the local weight system (Köhler and Ungnad, 1913: 325.2).

Luxury goods were imported into Judah. Excavations in and around the city have revealed the following imports: wood or wooden furniture from North Syria, ivory from Mesopotamia, decorative shells from the Red Sea, wine jars from Greece or Cyprus, fine pottery bowls from Assyria, scarabs from Egypt, and fish from the Mediterranean. Bronze ingots must have been imported from either Transjordan or Cyprus.

There is not much information on how all this trade was organised. Many biblical scholars assume that in the 10th century BCE (under Solomon) long-distance trade was simply a monopoly of the king and take it for granted that there would have been the same situation in the 7th century BCE. Some even presume that there were no Judahite merchants at all. Traders are often called 'Canaanites' in the Bible (as in the Hebrew of Zeph. 1:11) and this is taken to suggest that all merchants were foreigners. Perhaps, like 'gipsy' in modern English, the word could connote both a distinct ethnic group and distinctive economic activity.

There is indeed archaeological evidence for a large degree of centralisation in the production of exchange commodities in the 7th century BCE. Specialised settlements based on irrigation have been found along the coast of the Dead Sea connected with the large-scale exploitation of the balsam shrub (for perfume) and date palm; and the extraction of minerals such as salt and bitumen (asphalt). At En-Gedi, in the middle of that west coast, a small work-men's village has been excavated; and presumably it was connected with the production of these perfumes. Trade routes were protected by forts built along important roads. This all points to a well-organised and centralised approach to long-distance trade. Only the king could have managed this, with the help of a large bureaucracy. Our stories about Solomon date from later times. It may be that our image of his trading role derives from a literary back-projection on to the 10th century of this documented 7th century situation.

There are more archaeological indications for the centralisation of power. In Jerusalem, as elsewhere in Judah, stamped jar handles have been found in great quantities, dating from the 8th and the beginning of the 7th centuries BCE. The stamps consisted of a picture of a two- or four-winged beetle above which the letters *LMLK* can be read: *lamelek* – '(belonging) to the king' (Figure 25). These jars were presumably used to contain taxes paid to the crown in kind; and they will have contained the fruits of the land, be it grain, wine, or olive oil (Figure 26). Below the beetle were some other letters signifying place names, possibly the district capitals where the taxes were collected (although these names are not mentioned as such in the Bible).

The collection of taxes from the estates was thus standardised, or so it seems; and the same control was exercised over weighing. Just as in modern times, so too in 7th century Jerusalem weights were officially monitored. A total of 34 dome-shaped stone weights was found in one of the houses described in chapter 2. The standard, called *shekel*, was the equivalent of 11.34 gr. There were weights for 2, 4, 8, 16, 24 and 40 shekels; and quantities of less than one shekel – the gerah weights. Most frequent were the 8-shekel weights, which corresponded roughly to the Egyptian *deben*, and would have facilitated trade with Egypt (Scott 1985; TA 18/2).

Therefore, there is archaeological evidence to support the notion of a centralised administration and a well-developed bureaucracy. It is, however, too simple to presume that there were no Judahite merchants. There is an element in the archaeological evidence that points clearly to a more complicated situation: and that is the layout of the city. In the 10th century Jerusalem was quite straightforwardly an administrative centre, where only public buildings have been discovered; in the 7th century, however, the situation was different. The city had grown; but the additions were not of further palaces and storehouses. Excavations in the new areas, as already described in chapter 2,

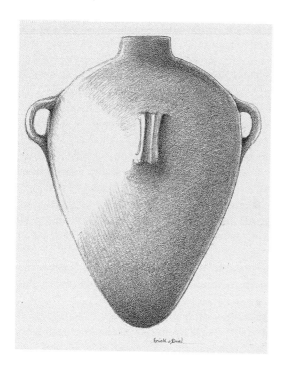

Figure 26
LMLK-jar, used to store
produce including wine
and olive oil.

Erick v Driel

have revealed almost exclusively the homes and working places of craftsmen and traders. Even the 'stepped stone structure', which had been part of a large fortification in the 'City of David', was being re-used as building space for houses. This may be taken as a sign of the increasing economic and thus political power for this segment of the population.

We cannot assume that these rich traders were all foreigners; there is nothing in the archaeological finds that confirms this idea. The pottery and most other objects were local, except for the imported luxuries described previously. The people living there probably had Judahite names: a Hebrew ostracon bearing the name Ahiel has been found in one of the houses (named thereafter the 'house of Ahiel'), as were the 'bullae' described below. One has to bear in mind, however, that the two ostraca with South Arabian names (see above) were also discovered nearby.

Thus although foreign trade was probably still organised by the king and the royal administration, local merchants may have had considerable influence on the process and will have shared in the revenues. After the campaign of the Assyrians at the end of the 8th century BCE every town of Judah except Jerusalem had been destroyed. Although some settlements did recover to a certain extent, many others were never repopulated. The balance of power in Judah was severely upset, enabling Jerusalem to become the largest city of Judah and even of Palestine. All power, economic and otherwise, had now been concentrated in Jerusalem, and it seems that merchants and administrators were co-operating in order to exploit the opportunities this offered.

Literary sources are not very helpful here. Very few inscriptions have been found in the excavated buildings, with one exception. As already mentioned in chapter 2, a collection of 51 'bullae' was discovered on the floor of a building of which only a small strip could be excavated (Shiloh 1986). 'Bullae' are imprints of personal seals on small lumps of clay, used to seal rolled papyri. Because the building had been on fire during the conflagration of the city in 587 BCE, the clay was baked hard, thus preserving the imprints of the seals very well. All the sealings consisted of names in early Hebrew script, in the form '(belonging) to X, son of Y'; and every seal was different. One even describes the owner as *hrp*, 'the doctor'. The names are certainly Judahite, but the only combination of names that can be found in the Bible is 'Gemariahu, son of Shaphan'. This (or another) Gemariahu is mentioned by Jeremiah (36:9-12) as 'Gemariah, the son of Shaphan, the scribe' (Figure 27).

According to Shiloh, the bullae did not come from a family archive, because then one would have expected more repetition of certain names. Therefore he interprets the building in which the bullae were found as a public building, part of the administration of the city. However, the other objects found in this 'bullae house' do not support this view. The bullae were found scattered amongst broken household pottery, and one would not expect to find cooking pots, stone weights, a bronze earring, an iron blade, and a pestle in an official archive. Since only a very small part of the floor was excavated, the lack of repetition of names is not conclusive. Given the nature of the other buildings in this area, it seems more plausible to interpret the 'bullae house' as the house of a trader, doing business with local people. The seals themselves, with which such impressions were made, are rarely found. One has been discovered in the

Figure 27   Bulla with impression of the seal of 'Elnathan, so[n] of Bilgai'.

destruction debris of the city (Prignaud 1964). It bears the name of 'Haggy, son of Yishal', a name not found on the bullae described above.

During Kenyon's excavations, three complete ostraca (inscribed pottery sherds) were discovered not on but below the floors of the bronze workshop described in chapter 2. These have been dated to the end of the 8th century (Lemaire 1978). The first one reads: '57 (jars) of oil, 4 (jars) of grain', while the second one mentions 'oil' several times as well as the figures '5' and '8' (jars of oil?). The third one is interesting because its three lines can be read as: '200; one has counted 18; to give a tithe'. This is the only inscription known where the 'tithe' is mentioned, a levy of 10% of the produce of an estate (Deut 14:22) – in this case apparently only of 9%: 18 out of 200. The ostraca are clearly of an administrative nature and show that olive oil was an important product of Judah.

The many excavations that have taken place in Jerusalem during the last 135 years have revealed only one complete house, dating from the 7th century BCE. It is located on the south-eastern hill, in the 'City of David', and is called the house of Ahiel by its excavators because two 'ostraca' bearing that name were found inside it (Shiloh 1984). This house tells us a lot about building techniques, decoration, and the living conditions of its occupants. The house of Ahiel was built on a precarious spot. In this area a large stone structure covering the slope of the hill had been erected in the 10th century BCE, functioning as a wall for the defence of the north-eastern corner of the town and as a substructure for a large 'royal' building on top of the hill (see chapter 2). Once a later city wall had been built lower down the hill this structure had no function any more in the defences of Jerusalem; and, when space became scarce in the town, terraces were cut into it to build houses on.

The house of Ahiel, which measured approximately 8 x 12 m., was built on such a terrace (Figure 28), and a small street ran alongside it. To reach the house one had to turn west into an alley, where a stone staircase led to a higher terrace. Here were located the entrances to two houses, the house of Ahiel on the right, another house on the left. These houses were well-built, with quoins and doorways of dressed limestone. In the debris of the house an ashlar was found which bore an incised inscription with two names: *lplth ls'ly* ('for [belonging to] Paltah, for Sa'li'). The entrance was one metre wide and presumably closed with a wooden door; some ironwork that may have held the wooden planks was found in the alley. The door opened into a pillared hall, partly roofed and partly open, leading to some utility rooms in the back. This hall was used as a storage and working place, while the family slept on the second floor. In one of the back rooms a toilet was discovered, as already mentioned in chapter 2. The small cell had an especially thick plaster floor,

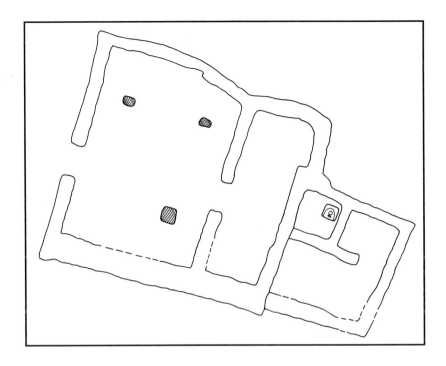

*Figure 28   Ahiel's house (see Figure 13) measured ca. 8 x 12m. The entrance (left)
leads through a courtyard with pillared side rooms into a back room.
Sleeping quarters were most probably located on the roof. In one of the
three small service rooms to the right a stone toilet seat was discovered
above a deep cesspit.*

with a stone seat embedded in a corner, located above a 2.60 m. deep cesspit.
Another room was used for storage; thirty-seven large jars were discovered
there. The floors of the building were made of thick layers of chalky white
plaster, and the stone walls were coated with the same plaster, which may have
been painted. Furniture has not been found, but in a neighbouring house several
pieces of charred wood were found, remains of furniture or decorations, which
were carved with palmette motifs. In other buildings so-called 'foot-baths'
were discovered in the hall large pottery basins used (so the interpretation
goes) for washing the feet upon entering the house (Figure 29). This was the
home of a rich family. Not only do the furnishings of their house attest to this,
but also the (little) information we have on their diet. In a stone-lined pit behind
one of the pillars were discovered 88 fishbones. These included bones from

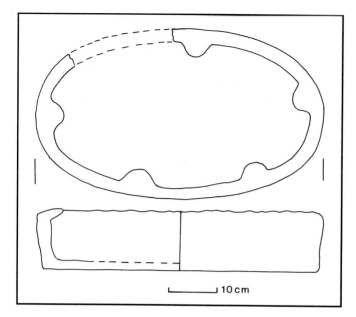

*Figure 29
Pottery foot-bath
found in the
courtyard of an
Iron Age house in
Jerusalem.*

10 cm

sea bream, caught in the Mediterranean, grey mullet from the coastal rivers, and Nile catfish living in the Yarkon river and the river Jordan. As all fish had to be imported to mountain-top Jerusalem, they must have been expensive.

We do not know what Ahiel's family did for a living. However, the workshop of the bronzesmith described in chapter 2 was situated in the same area, as was the 'bullae house' which contained the archive of a trader. The discovery in another building of some 120 loomweights, used in vertical looms, attests to commercial weaving activities (Figure 30). It may be assumed then that the heart of the old City of David housed a group of traders and artisans – and, considering the finds of Egyptian scarabs, bronze buckets, and even a fragment of an imported Greek wine jar, prosperous ones at that. This whole town quarter was well-planned, with stepped alleyways running east-west and north-south. Stone drains were discovered under some of these streets to carry off rainwater or refuse. Together with the use of toilets and foot-baths this gives an idea of the surprisingly high standard of hygiene in this part of the town.

From other parts of Jerusalem we have less or no information on the living conditions. Outside the city walls will have lived the poorer part of the population, including industrial workers like potters, fullers and tanners who needed a lot of space and water. There must have been a flourishing pottery industry around the city. Most excavated pots were made of local clays, and worked on a fast wheel – the work of specialised craftsmen. They made an undecorated but attractive light-red ware that is easily recognisable. Not only jugs and plates were made of pottery, clay being the cheapest material available, but also oil lamps and small statues that were used in cultic practices (see below). Clay was also the raw material for loomweights and sealings (*bullae*); but these were not oven-baked. As pottery sherds were abundant, spindle whorls and lids for jugs and jars were made from this waste material, and it was also used as writing material for ostraca. The pottery industry was located in the Hinnom Valley, according to the story found in Jeremiah 19, where Jeremiah

Figure 30   A vertical loom as used in Iron Age Palestine. Unbaked clay loomweights are attached to the warp threads.

Figure 31   A large storage jar, a jug for serving, a cooking pot, two storage bowls and several small bowls and plates made up the kitchen inventory of a Jerusalemite household.

is ordered to buy an earthenware jug. He then goes 'towards the Valley of Ben-hinnom as far as the Gate of the Potsherds'.

The enormous amount of pottery sherds excavated in Jerusalem may give some idea of the uses of the pots they represent (Figure 31). It turns out that the cooking pots were quite small, containing not more than 1.5-2 litres, and were much less abundant in the Iron Age than in the subsequent Roman and Byzantine periods. Lamps were also very sparse, as were small juglets for precious oils. Drinking cups did not exist, except for a small high bowl which we do not often find. In abundant supply were small bowls and platters for eating and drinking, and storage jars of different kinds. Bread ovens, which are found in every courtyard in smaller towns and villages, were almost completely absent in Jerusalem's quarters (as so far excavated). This repertoire tells us that cooking pots and lamps cannot have been in daily use. People probably ate bread (from

Figure 32
Bronze bucket with
bones of a mouse or
shrew found inside
it.

commercial bakers) with a paste made of chick peas or lentils, as they do today; and with olives, cheese, and fresh vegetables like onions and herbs. They may have roasted a sheep on festival days, and made some thick soup now and then.

Metal vessels, such as bronze cooking pots and silver drinking cups, will have been used by the very rich, but these have never been found; both fugitive and looter deemed them too valuable to leave behind for archaeologists. In the above-mentioned house of the many loomweights, some bronze buckets had been hidden in a hole in the wall, presumably in anticipation of the fall of the city. One of the buckets may have contained some grain, as the bones of a shrew or mouse were found in it, the poor animal having been trapped inside (Figure 32). Several iron hoes were hidden in the same place, testifying to the wealth these simple tools represented.

. . . and . . .

Religion was an important element in the life of the people. Besides the

Figure 33 A large cave filled with pottery and figurines was found near the Gihon spring. One of the walls of the small paved room blocks the entrance of Cave I, which may originally have been a tomb cut into bedrock.

Yahwistic religion and the official foreign cults mentioned in the Hebrew Bible, many forms of non-official beliefs existed among the common people. Archaeology has revealed some traces of these. In 1967, a large cave dating from the 8th century was discovered at the fringe of the City of David, near the Gihon spring (Figure 33) (Franken & Steiner 1990). It may originally have been used as a tomb, but did not function as such any more. It proved to be full of pottery (mainly dishes, platters and cooking pots – some of them still containing animal bones), and a great number of small pottery figurines as well. No precious objects were found at all: no jewellery, scarabs, imported luxury pottery, or metalwork. This practically rules out the possibility that this cave was a favissa, a repository for objects used in a temple, as the excavator had deduced. Apart from the fact that this would be the only favissa from the Iron Age ever found in Palestine, and that no temple has been found in the immediate vicinity, the cave can more easily be interpreted from its contents as a popular shrine of some sorts.

In antiquity caves were popular as shrines where one could make offerings to a deity and offer pledges for help; or as the seats of wise men and women, where one could go in case of despair. These 'holy (wo)men' knew ways to avert evil, procure healthy offspring, ward off sickness and barrenness, and please the gods. Even today it is not uncommon for the people of the region, especially the poorer ones, to go to such 'wise women' to ask for help, for instance in case of nightmares, even if they are devout Muslims or Christians.

It is possible that such a wise (wo)man lived in this cave – remains of a bread oven have been found inside – who was paid for services rendered with food, hence the many vessels. Or maybe food was offered there to an unknown deity or spirit, as names had been scratched on some vessels, possibly the names of the offerers. The figurines can be interpreted on the same level (Figure 34). Most were simple animal figurines: crudely made cows, and goats or sheep. Others were clearly horses, to judge from their forelock, and some even had riders on their backs. A disc was sometimes attached between the ears, although the difference from the aforementioned forelock is not always clear. This disc has been equated with the sun disc, thus implying a connection with the 'horses of the sun' mentioned in 2 Kings 23:11. This seems rather unlikely, as these 'horses of the sun', symbols of the Assyrian Sun God, were most likely beautiful

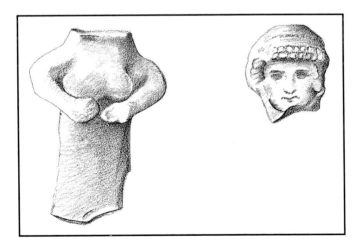

*Figure 34 Female figurine with pillar-like body and arms resting on
the belly. The head is mould-made. Both head and body
were originally painted with red and black stripes over a
white slip, suggesting make-up and clothing.*

statues, erected by the king at the entrance of the temple – unless, of course, they were models of such statues.

All in all, 38 fragments of miscellaneous animals were counted, as well as 21 horses, seven of them with riders. If that seems a large number, it is good to know that almost 560 figurines were discovered in Jerusalem by Kathleen Kenyon, and probably at least as many more in the later Israeli excavations. All figurines in the cave were broken, even if they were found next to complete vessels; and this implies that they had been destroyed on purpose.

It is the female figurines that have attracted most attention: mould-made heads attached to simple pillar-like bodies. Only thirteen pillared bodies and three heads were found in the cave. Although they are commonly described as naked women holding their breasts, careful analysis shows that this is not the case. Traces of whitewash have been detected on the bodies, over which lines have been painted in red and black, suggestive of clothing. The faces were enlivened with 'make-up', showing red cheeks and black lines around the eyes. As far as can be observed, the hands are not holding the breasts (which have the impression of being covered in cloth anyway) but are resting on the bellies. Attempts have been made to equate the female figurines with goddesses known from literature, but without success. The little statues simply lack divine attributes, and are rather to be interpreted as amulets or images of the women seeking help. Figurines of this kind, crudely made and apparently readily discarded, have been found in many towns in ancient Palestine, as well as in graves; and a comparable collection came from a shrine near Samaria, the capital of the northern kingdom Israel.

Of course we do not know which rituals took place in the cave, and the Bible is little help here as it barely recorded the devotion – or indeed other attitudes – of the common people. It is doubtful if the government did notice or mind these goings-on, or that the prophets much objected to this kind of popular religion; their real enemies were the official foreign cults, not simple popular beliefs.

It is interesting to note that no traces of cult practices have been found inside the excavated houses. Figurines are sometimes discovered on the floors and in the debris of the dwellings, but they do not seem to be connected with special rooms or cult installations. Nor have house altars been discovered. In the 7th century BCE religion seems to have been a 'communal' activity, practiced not at home but at separate cult sites, be it the Yahwistic temple or a cave-shrine – or even outside on the street. Note Jeremiah's complaint over the 'women of Jerusalem baking cakes in the streets of Jerusalem for the Queen of Heaven, (Jer 7:17-18).

Mention has to be made here of the many 'tumuli' found in the hills west of

Jerusalem, because they may have had religious significance. These tumuli are man-made structures, up to 7.5 m. high, in the shape of a truncated cone with a small flat area on top and steep slopes. Only three have ever been excavated, and only one of them completely (Amiran 1958). This structure was erected in two phases. First a low platform of red earth was formed with a stone pavement on top. A stone-lined pit nearby was filled with earth only and contained no sherds or bones. Next to the platform was a place where something had been burned. According to the description, it consisted of burnt debris, charcoal pieces, burnt animal bones, black earth saturated with fat, and blackened stones. Several pottery sherds from the 8th and 7th centuries BCE were found nearby. A stone ring wall with two entrances enclosed the area of the platform, stone-lined pit, and burning place. Ruth Amiran, who excavated the tumulus, concluded that the structure was used for a ritual connected with burning, be it cooking or sacrificing. The second phase consisted of the heaping up of the tumulus proper with loose stones. No human remains were found at all in the tumulus, nonetheless Amiran interpreted the structure as a tomb. Others rather see it as a 'high place' for worship (*bamah*). More excavations are certainly needed to solve the riddle of the tumuli of Jerusalem.

... Death

'So David slept with his fathers and was buried in the city of David', it says in 1 Kings 2:10, and thereafter every king was buried there. Somewhere in the City of David a royal sepulchre must have been located where the kings were laid to rest. Notable exceptions were King Uzziah, who was buried 'in the field of the burial of the kings, for they said: He is a leper' (2 Chron 26:23) and the later kings from Hezekiah onwards, who for some reason were buried elsewhere, be it 'the ascent of the sepulchres of the sons of David' (Hezekiah), or the 'garden of Uzza', which was also inside the city (Manasseh, Amon and probably Josiah). Three of the last four kings of Judah died in exile, the exception being Jehoiakim, who was probably buried in the 'garden of Uzza'.

The search for the royal necropolis was *the* incentive to start digging in Jerusalem in the 19th century. The first real excavation in the city took place in 1863 in the so-called 'Tomb of the Kings', now a well-known tourist site north of Damascus Gate. On behalf of the Louvre museum, F. de Saulcy cleared this ancient rock-cut tomb in the (mis)understanding that the 'Kings' buried there were the kings of Old Testament times. It turned out to be the burial ground of a rich family of the 1st century CE.

When continued archaeological research at the end of the 19th century showed that the city of David had been situated not on the western but on the

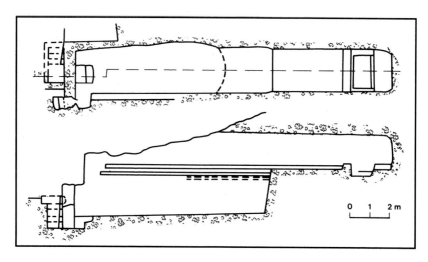

*Figure 35   Plan (above) and section (below) of a tunnel excavated by R. Weill, possibly
one of the royal tombs of the House of David. The section shows that the
upper tunnel ended in a depression, presumably for a sarcophagus. Later
(when the tomb became crowded?) a second tunnel was cut at a lower
level. Nothing was found inside the tunnels.*

south-eastern hill, the search was then concentrated there. In 1913 Raymond
Weill cleared the southern part of this hill down to bedrock during the first
large-scale excavations ever executed in Jerusalem. Unfortunately this area
had been used as a stone quarry in Roman times, thereby erasing every trace of
older buildings. Nonetheless Weill did find two long rock-cut tunnels, partly
damaged by the stone cutters and completely empty (Figure 35). According to
him these were the long sought-for royal tombs, robbed of their rich contents
in antiquity. Not many archaeologists agree with him nowadays, as the tunnels
are rather simple and sober, without inscriptions or decorations. As, however,
no other possible royal tombs have been discovered in the City of David, these
tunnels still stand as the only candidates.

The subjects of the Davidic kings were not buried inside the city. Up till
now more than 110 rock-cut tombs from the Iron Age have been discovered
and excavated in Jerusalem, all outside the City of David. It is difficult to date
them precisely, because most are found empty, but similar graves were common
in the 9th to the 7th centuries BCE.

North of the Damascus Gate, not far from the above-mentioned 'Tomb of
the Kings', a cemetery was found with several large tombs. Two were discovered
on the property of the Monastery of St Etienne, which houses the famous École

Biblique (Barkay and Kloner 1986). Both tombs displayed the same characteristics. Complex 2 is illustrated in Figure 36. It probably served as a family tomb for one of the rich trading families. Around a large central (underground) courtyard, four burial chambers were situated with stone benches for the bodies of the deceased. Headrests were also cut out of the stone, showing that two bodies could occupy the same bench. Underneath the benches were 'repositories' for the burial goods. A small side room may have been used for dressing and anointing the body before it was laid to rest. Since this tomb had been robbed in antiquity, like almost every tomb in Jerusalem, nothing was found inside it.

Two similar tombs, discovered and excavated in 1937, have been published by A. Mazar (1976). They were located on the slope of the hill just north of the Damascus Gate, not far from the so-called Garden Tomb. That rock-cut tomb was found in 1867 by a local peasant during repair works, and 'identified' not much later by General Charles George Gordon (of Khartoum) as the grave of Jesus. Many still venerate it as such, although its similarity to the above-

Figure 36 This large family tomb found north of Damascus Gate has several burial chambers with stone benches. The room without benches may have been used to dress and anoint the body of the deceased.

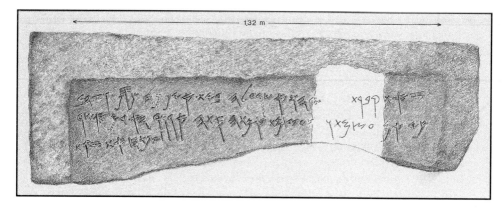

*Figure 37 Inscription engraved in the facade of the 'Tomb of the Royal Steward'
[after Ussishkin 1993, ill. 18.3].*

mentioned tombs suggests a much earlier date in the Iron Age.

Another necropolis was discovered in the Arab village Silwan, opposite the City of David. Some fifty graves were found there, different in design from the above-mentioned necropolis, because each tomb had only one sepulchre chamber. Among them were three 'monolithic' tombs, completely hewn out of the rock. The most famous one is known as the 'Tomb of the Daughter of the Pharaoh'. The other two have burial inscriptions over the entrance, of which only one is still readable (Figure 37). Prof. N. Avigad translated this one as: '[the tomb of . . .]yahu, who is over the house. There is no silver and gold here but rather [his bones] and the bones of his wife (?) with him. Cursed be the man who should open this.' The warning had no effect; the tomb was empty and in use as a water cistern. A connection has been made with Isaiah's invective against one of the ministers or chamberlains of the court: Shebna (short for Shebnayahu), who also was 'over the house', which described a high governmental office. Isaiah suggests that Shebna was a foreigner: 'What have you to do here and who have you here, you who hew a tomb on the height, and carve a habitation for yourself in the rock?' (Is 22:16).

If this tomb indeed belonged to Shebna, then maybe we should interpret the whole complex as the burialground of officials, many of whom came from abroad and were therefore buried not in their far-away family tombs, but in single graves, cut out for them personally and maybe for their wives. D. Ussishkin, who has recently published the necropolis (1993), could find no Israelite parallels for architectural features such as the gabled roofs and cornices which characterised many of the tombs. These features could only be traced

Figure 38
Drawing of the inscription on a
silver plaque found in a grave at
Ketef Hinnom.

quite far away – in Urartu, Phrygia, Lydia (all three in modern Turkey), Cyprus, and Etruria (Tuscany). Other tombs displayed clear Egyptian influence. An intriguing indication is the fact that, contrary to the family tomb mentioned above, the benches in these tombs are all of different sizes, as if indeed they were 'made to measure'.

During the excavations near the Temple Mount, carried out by Benjamin Mazar, some rock-cut installations from the Iron Age were discovered. These were underground chambers without benches, accessible by means of a vertical shaft. Each chamber also had a rectangular 'chimney' in its ceiling. Mazar interpreted these installations as tombs because of their similarity to the Phoenician tombs found in Achziv (Mazar and Mazar 1989).

How rich all these tombs may have been originally can be deduced from the tombs, already mentioned in chapter 2, that were found near the Scots Kirk, outside the medieval Old City towards the railway station in the south-west. This is the only burial ground so far found that had not been robbed; and among the finds were gold and silver jewellery, ivory ornaments, and cosmetic palettes (Barkay 1986). The most exciting discovery, however, was two small silver plaques, 97 x 27 and 39 x 11 mm. in size (Figure 38). Engraved with a fine pen were short rolled-up texts each including seventeen or eighteen lines. These are by no means all legible; but both appear to include a shorter version of the so-called Aaronic blessing preserved in Numbers 6:24-26 – a version which does not include the familiar italicised words:

Yahweh bless you and keep you

Yahweh make his face (or 'countenance') shine on you *and be gracious to you*

Yahweh lift up his ('face' or) countenance on you and give you peace.

In one of them, a line or two higher up, some other words also found in the Bible (in Deut 7:9 and Solomon's prayer, 1 Kings 8:23) have been detected: '[keeping] the covenant [and the] loyalty for . . .' (Yardeni 1991). There are of course commentators who have hailed these as the oldest evidence we have for the biblical text. However, several other points can be more reliably made: they provide our earliest testimony to a benediction current at least in the monarchic period which became incorporated in somewhat longer form in the traditions of Moses; they provide further early evidence for the use of the proper name of the Bible's God, Yahweh; and since, as rolled up in the silver jewellery, they may have functioned as charms or amulets, they are an early illustration of what developed into Jewish *tefillin* – the little boxes containing scriptural passages and worn on arm and forehead.

One should realise that the tombs so far discovered represent the burial grounds of the 'rich and mighty'. Indeed the tombs at Ketef Hinnom may have belonged to a rich priestly family. It is difficult to imagine that the lower classes of Jerusalem could afford such elaborate constructions. We must rather assume that they were buried in simple graves, dug into the ground, further away from the city and the temple. This could be the reason that their graves have not yet been detected and probably never will be.

5

Visiting Ancient Jerusalem

If this is the last chapter you are reading in this book, you will already know – and if this is the first, then it has to be admitted at the outset – that remarkably few details of oldest Jerusalem are still available for inspection. The movable ones that do remain are mostly displayed in Jerusalem's own museums: pre-eminently in the Israel Museum in the public heart of the western part of the modern city. This short chapter is not intended as a replacement for the relevant portions of the two excellent guides by Murphy O'Connor (1980, 3rd edition 1992) and Prag (1989). The ancient locations themselves are all much changed; but the visitor does have two ways available by which they can be appreciated better.

The one is to visit either by road transport or, more energetically, on foot some of the surrounding vantage points with longer views. One might start with the western perimeter road round the Hebrew University campus on Mount Scopus, for the best view from the north-east (preferably in later afternoon), or with the top of the Mount of Olives (at any time of day), for the view from due east, of the site of the ancient acropolis which once contained the temple and king's house. The visitor must just remember that the ancient raised platform, however impressive in its time, was much smaller than the vast space now occupied by the two great Muslim shrines and their attendant buildings.

The best views of the most ancient lower city are from the south (like the aerial view on the front cover of this book). A more distant one is from an outlook point near the local United Nations headquarters at the former British 'Government House'. An excellent closer view is obtained on the road east from the railway station that picks its winding way down, mostly east and a little north, through Abu Tor, to where the three valleys meet south of the pool of Siloam. From that road one can glimpse something of the shape of the oldest city. One has to remember that the valley on its left/west was much deeper then, and that the smaller ancient platform on the holy summit had obtruded rather less than Herod's expansion now does. Nowadays, there is rather little housing on that lower hill. To get an impression of how it looked in ancient

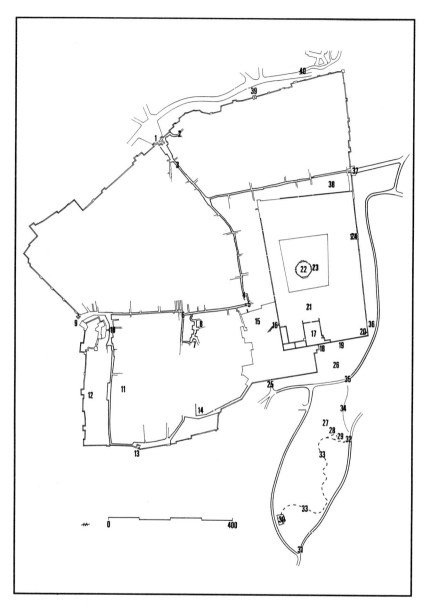

Figure 39   Plan of Jerusalem.

84

times we have first to inspect from this distance the modern Arab village of Silwan that hugs the eastern side of the Kidron Valley, and then to let our mind's eye carry it over to the more empty hill on the west side.

The other tour can be done only on foot – round the actual perimeter of the ancient city. We recommend that you walk counter-clockwise, like the description in Nehemiah 3 of the rebuilding of the walls (cf chapter 1). The numbers within square brackets in the paragraphs that follow provide the key to the numbers on the map of Jerusalem (Figure 39). A good place to start is the Damascus Gate in the north wall of today's 'Old City' [1]. Either climb on to its roof, or find a vantage point up the first stepped lane just inside the gate to the left [2], and look slightly east of southwards into the city: you can still see at roof-top height the line of the ancient valley down which you are to walk, between the lesser height of the sacred area to the left/east, and the greater height of the Mishneh or Upper City to the right/west.

Leave the walls and follow Valley (or *al-Wad*) Street south [3]. You could continue on that line passing under the main west-east axis of the 'Old City' leading from the Jaffa Gate [9] to the Dome of the Rock [22] to the Western (or Wailing) Wall [15], straight out of today's 'Old City' by the Dung Gate[25], and down the motor road to the Pool of Siloam [30]; and, if you did so, you would be walking a little way outside the west walls of Nehemiah's time. And, at least as long as you were still in the medieval 'Old City', you would be walking just below the west walls of the acropolis of Jerusalem in the time of her earlier kings. But, if time is short and everything must be done on the one walk, then two 'detours' are necessary additions.

When you reach the main west-east axis, you will be close to the ancient Ephraim Gate. Mount the steps on the left [4]; then turn right, up the Street of the Chain [5], and you will be walking just north of today's 'Jewish Quarter' – and also of the 7th century BCE 'Mishneh'. Turn left, half-way up, into Jewish Quarter Road [6]. Remains from several periods have been incorporated into or under the new buildings. You will easily find the Byzantine 'Cardo' (main north/south street) and a Crusader market; and you can visit nearby the impressive portion of early 7th century city wall exposed by Avigad [7]. Just to the north of it as you return to the Street of the Chain you can see the remains of a tower, part of a wall from later in that century [8]. Return to the main axis [6], and continue west to just inside the Jaffa Gate [9].

Visit the Citadel [10], which houses a museum showing the history of Jerusalem from the earliest times. In the courtyard of the Citadel, excavations have yielded remains from the Hellenistic period onwards. Be sure to visit the cellar of the Citadel, where there is an interesting model of Jerusalem in the 19th century (CE). And if you then follow the motor road south from the Citadel, inside the present walls, through the Armenian Quarter [11] to where it ends south of the Jewish Quarter [14], we think that you will have remained outside the 7th century Mishneh wall found by Avigad. Maximalists, who are well represented in Jerusalem itself, extend the Mishneh in this period west to the present west wall, and further south than the present south wall. However, Tushingham's excavations with Kenyon to the west of that road, in the site of the modern Armenian Seminary [12], disclosed evidence of quarrying in our period – but no structures till Herodian or Roman times. The same is true of Broshi's excavations outside the Zion Gate, which you will have passed near the south-west corner by the summit of the south-western hill [13]. He excavated one house from the First Temple period, with pottery and figurines in context; but that of course does not imply that this area now called 'Mount Zion' was inside the city walls in the time of Judah's kings. Near the end of the motor road, you can look for houses from the Herodian period and the huge apse of the Nea Church of Byzantine times [14], all of which have been turned into museums. And look for the Rachel Ben Zvi Centre for the study of ancient Jerusalem. A large topographical maquette has been erected showing the remains of Jerusalem in Hebrew Bible times, as far as these have been exposed in excavations. Pick your way from the upper part of the Jewish Quarter to the open plaza in front of the Western Wall [15], and you will have rejoined the valley you were walking down from the Damascus Gate.

The next 'detour' really takes you to the heart of things. Enter the *Haram al-Sharif* (or 'Temple Mount') by the ramp up to the Maghrabi (or Moors) Gate [16]. In front of the great Aqsa mosque to your right [17], note the steps that descend below it, and would have led in Herod's time to the older lower city. The present ramp leads to the Double Gate of the early Islamic period, now sealed up, inside which remains a vestibule with Herodian features [18]. Further east, in this south wall of the Haram, is the Triple Gate [19]. And just inside the south-east corner, there are steps which take one down to 'Solomon's Stables' [20].

Walk from the Aqsa mosque northwards, up to the Dome of the Rock. You pass the great water fountain [21], where Muslim worshippers wash before praying, and below which there are huge reservoirs of water fed in Herodian times and till much more recently by aqueducts from near Bethlehem and as far as Hebron to the south. Visit the Dome of the Rock [22], for the sake of the monument itself of course – but also to see the ancient rock which it celebrates, on or near which the most holy innermost part of the ancient temple may have been. Note the much smaller Dome of the Chain [23], nearby to the east, almost precisely at the intersection of the diagonals of the present sacred area. We have suggested this structure might mark the position of the ancient great altar of sacrifice. As you look north from there, or from the platform on which the Dome of the Rock stands, remember that even in Herod's time – let alone in the period we have been reviewing – the sacred area did not extend so far north of 'the Rock'. Then, on the eastern wall, and a little further to the north, note the position of the Golden Gate [24], also sealed from the outside. Return to the Plaza via the Moors' Gate [16].

On leaving the 'Old City' by the Dung Gate [25], make for the motor road going downhill to the Pool of Siloam [30]. Note first the archaeological park a little way to the left [26]. The remains are mainly from Herodian and Byzantine times. A large building and gate from the 9th century BCE have been excavated here, but they are difficult to trace among the many walls from later periods. Above you, on the 'Old City' wall, you will see the sealed-up Double [18] and Triple [19] Gates. Not far outside the Dung Gate, on the road downhill, a further archaeological garden has been laid out, showing the results of the excavations by the Hebrew University of Jerusalem (1968-85), directed by the late Yigal Shiloh. Here too M. Parker, R.A.S. Macalister, and Kathleen Kenyon dug; and, wherever possible, architectural remains from their excavations are included in the display. The impressive remains of the stepped stone structure from the 10th century BCE and the 12th century terraces below it are visible [27]. On top are reconstructions of houses from the late 7th century BCE, including the 'house of Ahiel'. And, from later periods, a Persian city wall and tower and a large Maccabean tower can be seen.

Lower down the slope, and no longer within the archaeological garden, are the remains of the oldest city wall of Jerusalem, from the Middle Bronze Age (about 1800 BCE), as well as of the Iron Age city wall from the 7th century BCE. However, these are difficult to find, as the area is a rubbish dump [28]. Close by is located the entrance from above (from inside the city) to the water systems of ancient Jerusalem: Warren's Shaft, the underground tunnel to the spring [29]. Steeply downhill to the east is the entrance to Hezekiah's Tunnel [33] which brings the water from Gihon by a winding course of some 544m to Siloam at the southernmost end of the ancient city. In the southern part of the city, more remains from Shiloh's excavations have been exposed, mostly from the Hellenistic and later periods, although parts of the already-mentioned city wall from the Middle Bronze and Iron Ages have been revealed here as well. Return to the motor road down the higher, western valley as far as the Pool of Siloam [30], where you meet the lower Kidron valley.

From the Pool of Siloam, walk up the Kidron valley [31] to the beginning of Hezekiah's Tunnel at the Virgin's Fountain [33] (or, if you are not claustrophobic, walk through up the tunnel [32]). Then leave the road for the steep pathway [34] towards the Aqsa mosque and the Dung Gate. When you reach the upper motor road, follow it northwards [35], outside the east wall of the city and the *Haram*. Just north of the south-east corner, before the gate to the Muslim cemetery [36], note the impressive evidence of a join in the east wall, where a southerly extension of the platform had been made. Observe the outside of the Golden Gate [24] as you pass, and re-enter the 'Old City' by St Stephen's (or the Lions') Gate [37]. To your left, just inside that gate, is the *birket Israil* (The 'Pool of Israel') [38]. Somewhere nearby had been the location of the ancient Sheep Pool, to the south of which – and within the present Haram – had been the Sheep Gate of biblical times. The Sheep Gate and Pool of Herodian times was further north, in fact on the north side of the motor road from the gate which will take you westwards back to Valley Street [3], well to the north of the ancient north wall.

Return to the Damascus Gate [1], and follow the main road eastwards along the north wall till you come, beyond Herod's Gate, to the entrance on your left to the Rockefeller Museum [40]. You will find displayed there some finds from Parker's excavations: bowls and jugs from the Early Bronze Age.

In the Israel Museum, in the heart of western Jerusalem, much more material is exhibited from the Jerusalem we have been reviewing. A large proto-Ionic capital from the 10th century BCE can be found; the luxury objects from the Ketef Hinnom tomb, including the engraved silver amulets; the engraved ivory pomegranate; and the finds from Shiloh's excavations in the City of David. Also a reconstructed window balustrade has been erected from the palace at Ramat Rahel.

Literature

Aharoni, Y., 1979, *The Land of the Bible. A Historical Geography* (2nd ed), Burns & Oates, London.

Amiran, R., 1958, 'The Tumuli West of Jerusalem: Surveys and Excavations, 1953'; *Israel Exploration Journal* 8; pp205-27.

Ariel, D.T., 1990, *Excavations at the City of David 1978-1985*, Vol. II: *Imported Stamped Amphora Handles, Coins, Worked Bone and Ivory, and Glass* (Qedem, 30), Jerusalem.

Asali, K.J. (ed.), 1989, *Jerusalem in History*, Scorpion, Buckhurst Hill.

Auld, A.G., 1994, *Kings without Privilege. David and Moses in the Story of the Bible's Kings*, T&T Clark, Edinburgh.

Avigad, N., 1983, *Discovering Jerusalem*, Thomas Nelson, Nashville.

Barkay, G., 1986, *Ketef Hinnom. A Treasure facing Jerusalem's Walls*, The Israel Museum, Jerusalem.

Barkay, G. and A. Kloner, 1986, 'Jerusalem Tombs from the First Temple', *Biblical Archaeology Review* XII, pp22-39.

Barkay, G., 1990 'A Late Bronze Age Egyptian Temple in Jerusalem', *Eretz Israel*, 21, pp94-106 (Hebrew).

Bliss, F.J. and A.C. Dickie, 1989 *Excavations at Jerusalem, 1894-1897*, Palestine Exploration Fund, London.

Blok, H. and M.L. Steiner, 1991, *De onderste steen boven. Opgravingen in Jeruzalem*, Kok, Kampen.

Busink, T.A., 1970/80, *Der Tempel von Jerusalem*, 2 vols, Brill, Leiden.

Cahill, J., K. Reinhard, D. Tarlor and P. Warnock; 1991, 'It Had to Happen: Scientists Examine Remains of Ancient Bathroom', *BAR* 17, pp64-69.

Cowley, A.E., 1923, *Aramaic Papyri of the Fifth Century BC*, Clarendon Press, Oxford.

Crowfoot, J.W. and G.M. Fitzgerald, 1929, *Excavations in the Tyropoean Valley, Jerusalem, 1927* (PEF Annual, 5), Palestine Exploration Fund, London.

Davies, G.I., 1991, *Ancient Hebrew Inscriptions: corpus and concordance*, Cambridge University Press.

Davies, P.R. (ed.), 1993, *Second Temple Studies* (JSOT Suppl.117), Sheffield Academic Press, Sheffield.

De Groot, A. and D.T. Ariel (eds), 1992, *Excavations at the City of David 1978-1985*; Vol. III: *Stratigraphical, Environmental, and other Reports* (Qedem, 33), Jerusalem.

Franken, H.J., 1969, *Excavations at Tell Deir Alla*, Vol. I, Brill, Leiden.

Franken, H.J. and M.L. Steiner, 1990, *Excavations in Jerusalem 1961-1967*; Vol. II: *The Iron Age Extramural Quarter on the South-East Hill* (British Academy Monographs in Archaeology, 2), Oxford University Press for the British Academy and the British School of Archaeology in Jerusalem, Oxford.

Gill, D., 1991, 'Subterranean Waterworks of Biblical Jerusalem: Adaptation of a Karst System', *Science*, 254, 1467-70.

Hamilton, R.W., 1942/43, 'Excavations against the North Wall of Jerusalem, 1937-38', *Quarterly of the Department of Antiquities in Palestine*, 10, pp 1-53.

Hamilton, R.W., 1950, 'The Citadel, Jerusalem: A Summary of Work since 1934', *Quarterly of the Department of Antiquities in Palestine*, 14, pp121-189.

Horwitz, L.K., 1989, 'Diachronic Changes in Rural Husbandry Practices in Bronze Age Settlements from the Refaim Valley, Israel', *PEQ*, 121, pp 44-54.

Kallai, Z., 1986, *Historical Geography of the Bible. The Tribal Territories of Israel*, Magnes, Jerusalem; Brill, Leiden.

Kenyon, K.M., 1967, *Jerusalem. Excavating 3000 Years of History* (New Aspects of Antiquity), Thames and Hudson, London.

Kenyon, K.M., 1974, *Digging up Jerusalem*, Benn, London.

King, P.J., 1992 'Jerusalem', D.N. Freedman (ed.), *Anchor Bible Dictionary*, Doubleday, New York.

Köhler, J. and A. Ungnad, 1913, *Assyrische Rechtsurkunde in Umschnft und Übersetzung*, Leipzig.

Lemaire,A., 1978, 'Les Ostraca Paléo-Hébreux des Fouilles de l'Ophel', *Levant* X, pp156-60.

Macalister, R.A.S. and J.G. Duncan, 1926, *Excavations on the Hill of Ophel, Jerusalem, 1923-1925* (PEF Annual, 4), Palestine Exploration Fund, London.

Mazar, A., 1990, 'Iron Age Burial Caves North of the Damascus Gate', *Israel Exploration Journal* 26; pp1-8.

Mazar, A., 1990, *Archaeology of the Land of the Bible 10,000-586 B.C.E.*, The Lutterworth Press, Cambridge.

Mazar, E., and B. Mazar, 1989, *Excavations in the South of the Temple Mount: The Ophel of Biblical Jerusalem* (Qedem, 29), Hebrew University, Jerusalem.

Mazar, E., 1989, 'Royal Gateway to Ancient Jerusalem Uncovered', *Biblical Archaeology Review* 15, pp38-51.

Miller, J.M., 1974, 'Jebus and Jerusalem: a Case of Mistaken Identity', *Zeitschrift des Deutschen Palästina-Vereins* 90, pp115-127.

Millard, A.R., 1989, 'Does the Bible Exaggerate King Solomon's Golden Wealth?', *Biblical Archaeology Review* 15, pp20-31.

Murphy-O'Connor, J., 1992, *The Holy Land. An Archaeological Guide from Earliest Times to 1700* (3rd ed.), Oxford University Press.

Otto, E., 1980, *Jerusalem - die Geschichte der Heiligen Stadt, von den Anfängen bis zur Kreuzfahrerzeit* (Urban-Taschenbücher 308), Kohlhammer, Stuttgart.

Prag, K., 1989, *Jerusalem* (Blue Guides), A&C Black, London.

Prignaud, J., 1964, 'Un Sceau Hébreu de Jérusalem et un ketib du Livre d'Esdras', *Revue Biblique* LXXI, pp372-83.

Pritchard, J. B. (ed.), 1974, *Ancient Near Eastern Texts relating to the Old Testament* (3rd ed.), Princeton University Press.

Purvis, J.D., 1988, *Jerusalem, the Holy City. A Bibliography* (ATLA Bibliography Series, 20), The Scarecrow Press, London.

Robinson, E. and E. Smith, 1860, *Biblical Researches in Palestine and the Adjacent Regions: Journal of Travels in the Year 1838* (2nd ed.)., John Murray, London.

Saller, S.J., 1964, *The Excavations at Dominus Flevit (Mount Olivet, Jerusalem)*; Part II: *The Jebusite Burial Place*, Jerusalem.

de Saulcy, L.F.C., 1882, *Jérusalem*, Morel, Paris.

Scott, R.B.Y., 1985, 'Weights from the 1961-1967 Excavations', Tushingham (1985), pp197-212.

Shiloh, Y., 1984, *Excavations at the City of David I: 1978-1982* (Qedem 19), The Hebrew University, Jerusalem.

Shiloh, Y., 1985, 'The Material Culture of Judah and Jerusalem in Iron Age II: Origins and Influences', E. Lipinski (ed.), *The Land of Israel, Crossroad of Civilisations*, pp113-146, Peeters, Leuven.

Shiloh, Y., 1986, 'A Group of Hebrew Bullae from the City of David', *Israel Exploration Journal* 36, pp16-38.

Simons, J., 1952, *Jerusalem in the Old Testament: Researches and Theories*, Brill, Leiden.

Smith, G.A., 1894, *Historical Geography of the Holy Land*, Hodder and Stoughton, London.

Smith, G.A., 1907/8, *Jerusalem, from the Earliest Times to 70 A.D.*, 2 Vols, Hodder and Stoughton, London.

Steiner, R.C., 1989, 'New Light on the Biblical Millo from Hatran Inscriptions', *Bulletin of the American Schools of Oriental Research*, 276, pp15-23.

Tushingham, A.D., 1985, *Excavations in Jerusalem 1961-1967*, Vol. I, Royal Ontario Museum, Toronto; Brill, Leiden.

Ussishkin, D.,1993, *The Village of Silwan: The Necropolis from the Period of the Judean Kingdom*, Israel Exploration Society, Jerusalem.

de Vaux, R., 1962-64, 'Jérusalem (Ophel)', *Revue Biblique*; 69, pp98-100; 70, pp416-9; 71, pp253-8.

Vincent, L.H., 1911, *Jérusalem sous terre: Les récentes fouilles d'Ophel*, Horace Cox, London.

Vincent, L.H., 1912, *Jérusalem: Recherches de topographie, d'archéologie et d'histoire, I. Jérusalem antique*, Gabalda Paris.

Warren, C., 1976, *Underground Jerusalem: An Account of Some of the Principal Difficulties Encountered in its Exploration and the Results Obtained*, Bentley, London.

Weill, R., 1920, *La Cité de David. Compte rendu des fouilles exécutées à Jérusalem, sur le site de la ville primitive. Campagne de 1913-1914*, Geuthner, Paris.

Weill, R., 1947, *La Cité de David. Compte rendu des fouilles exécutées à Jérusalem, sur le site de la ville primitive. Campagne de 1923-1925*, Geuthner, Paris.

Weippert, H., 1988, *Palästina in vorhellenistischer Zeit*, Handbuch der Archäologie, Vorderasien II/1, C.H. Beck, München.

Wilkinson, J., 1974, 'Ancient Jerusalem: Its Water Supply and Population', *Palestine Exploration Quarterly*, 106, pp33-51.

Williamson, H.G.M., 1984 'Nehemiah's Walls Revisited', *Palestine Exploration Quarterly*, 116, pp81-88.

Wilson, C.W. and C. Warren, 1871, *The Recovery of Jerusalem: A Narrative of Exploration and Discovery in the City and the Holy Land*, Bentley, London.

Yardeni, A., 1991, 'Remarks on the priestly blessing on two ancient amulets from Jerusalem', *Vetus Testamentum*, 41, pp176-185.

Index

Aaronic Blessing 82
Abdi-Khiba 28-9
Abraham 52
acropolis 20, 83, 85
Aharoni, Y. 61,89
Ahaz, King 14
Ahiel 30, 66, 68-70, 87
Alexander the Great xi, 47
altar 15,52, 57, 60, 76, 87
Armana [Letters] 28-9
Amenhotep III 29
Amiran, R. 77, 89
al-Aqusa 49, 86, 88
Arab 63
Arad 57
Arauna 14
Ariel, D.T. 10, 26, 89-90
Artaxerxes 47
Asa 20, 60
Asali, K.J. 89
Ashkelon 37
Assyria[n] 39, 42-3, 60, 63, 75
Athaliah 19
Auld, A.G. 11-12, 54, 89
Avigad, N. 6, 10, 41, 80, 85-6, 89

Babylon 11, 13, 37, 42, 44-5, 53, 57, 59-61, 63-4
bamah 77
Barkay, G. 30,46, 78, 82, 89
bayt al-maqdis 1
Bethlehem 61
Beth-shean 29-30
biblical archaeology 9
bit hilani 58
Bliss, F.J. 6, 7, 89

Blok, H. 89
Boaz 54
British School of Archaeology xi, 9
Bronze Age 22-33
Broshi, M. 86
bullae 30, 42, 66-7, 71
Busink, T.A. 89
Byzantine Cardo 10, 85

Cahill, J. 45, 90
'Canaanites' 64
cemetery – see tomb[s]
Cheesemongers'Valley 21
Chronicles 11-12, 20, 33-4, 39, 52
Citadel 8, 40, 85
Cowley, A.E. 47, 90
crossroads 4
Crowfoot, J.W. 6, 8, 90
cultic objects 39, 53, 57
Cyprus 57-9, 64
Cyrus 45

Damascus 62-3
Damascus Gate 8, 18, 30, 77-9, 85, 88
David 11-14, 20, 21-2, 33, 47, 53, 59-60, 77; city of 2, 13-15, 21, 33, 51, 63, 66, 68, 70, 74, 77-8, 88; tomb of 2, 4, 33, 78
Davies, G.I. 90
Davies, P.R. 43, 90
De Groot, A. 10, 90
Dier Alla 57
Deuteronomy 59
Dickie, A.C. 6, 7, 89
diet 45, 69-70, 72-3
Dome of the Chain 52, 62, 86
Dome of the Rock 49, 51-2, 62, 86-7

Dragon Shaft   26, 87
Duncan, J.G.

Early Bronze Age [EBA]   21-2
Echnaton   29
École Biblique   8, 78
Egypt[ian]   xi, 15-6, 27-30, 32, 39, 60, 65, 81
Ekron   41
Execration Texts   27

favissa   74
figurines   39, 75-6
Fitzgerald, G.M.   90
Franken, H.J.   10, 39, 57, 74, 90

gate [names] of biblical Jerusalem
Benjamin [Upper?]   18-20; Corner   16, 18-20, 39-40; East   17; Ephraim   16, 18, 20, 85; Fish   17; Horses   17-19; Middle   18-19; Mishneh   17; New   18-19; Old [City]   17; Potsherd   18-19; Refuse, or Dung   17, 19, 85, 87; Sheep   17-19; Spring   17; Upper   16, 20; Valley   17, 19, 39; Watch   17-18, 60; Water   17-18
Gaza   29
Gedaliah   45
Gihon   17, 22-3, 29, 32, 35, 40, 42-4, 74
Gill, D.   26, 42-3, 90
Giloh   33
Golden Gate   18, 51, 87-8
goldsmiths   17-18, 60

Hamilton, R.W.   6, 8, 90
Har ha-Bayit   49
al-Ḥaram al-Sharif   7, 10, 18, 20, 49-51, 86, 88
Hazor   24, 37, 55, 57
Helena, Empress   4
Hellenistic   8, 46, 85
Herod, King   8, 9, 47, 49-51, 53, 83, 86
Hezekiah, King   14, 20, 39-40, 42-4, 7, 87
Hinnom, valley of   19
Hiram of Tyre   12, 59
Holy of Holies   52, 55
Horwitz, L.K.   27, 90
'house of Yahweh'   15, 20

Huldah   16

Intermediate Period   23
Iron Age [IA]   232, 40, 45, 70, 72, 74, 78, 87
Israel/ites   4, 11-4, 16, 20, 33, 39, 51, 60, 76
Israel Museum   83, 88

Jachin   54, 57
Jaffa Gate   8, 41, 85
Jebus/ite[s]   8, 13-14, 33
Jeremiah   18, 60, 67, 71, 76
Joash, King   13
Johns, C.N.   6, 8
Josephus   2, 8, 21-2, 40, 53
Josiah   16, 20
Jotham   40
Judah   4, 11-2, 15, 33, 39, 42, 45, 47, 57, 59, 62, 66-7

Kallai, Z.   61, 91
Kenyon, Kathleen M.   6, 9, 10, 26, 29, 32, 40-1, 68, 76, 86-7, 91
Ketef Hinnom   45, 81, 88
Kidron   4, 19-20, 21-2, 85, 87
King, Phillip J.   4, 7, 91
King's Garden   19
Kloner, A.   78, 89
Kohler, J.   64, 91

Lachish   35, 51
Late Bronze Age [LBA]   29-33
Lebanon/ese   12, 59
Lemaire, A.   68, 91
LMLK jars   65-6
loom   71
luxury [goods]   61, 64, 66, 74

Macalister R.A.S.   6, 8, 10, 87, 91
Maccabean   8, 30, 87
Maktesh   39
Manasseh   40
Mazar, A.   79, 91
Mazar, B.   6, 9-10, 38, 81, 91
Mazar, E.   10, 38, 81, 91
Megiddo   29, 35
Melchizedek   15

Biblical Passages

Genesis		9:1, 10	54	15:16	20	
14:18	15	9:15	13, 34	23:15	19	
22	52	9:20	14	24:25	13	
		9:24	13, 15	29:9-10	40	
Numbers		10:17-21	54-5	26:23	77	
6:24-26	82	11:1	54	27:3	16, 40	
		11:27	13, 15	29:16	20	
Deuteronomy		15:13	20	30:14	20	
7:9	82	20:34	63	32:3-5	43	
14:22	68			32:5	15, 40	
		2 Kings		33:14	15, 16, 40	
Josuah		11:16	19	36:18-19	60	
15:59	61	12:20	13			
		18:17	42	Ezra		
Judges		22:14	20	1:2-4	45	
9:6, 20	13	23:4-20	20	3:12	62	
19:10-11	14	23:11	75	6:3	46	
		25:3	44			
2 Samuel		25:10-12	45	Nehemiah		
5:6-9	13-14	25:13-17	61	2:11-16	16, 47	
5:8	2			2:14	42	
5:9,12	15			3:1-32	16-18, 85	
6:12	15	1 Chronicles		3:14	61	
15:13	20	11:4-8	13	3:15	15, 19	
24:16, 18	14	11:4-5	14	3:26-7	16	
		15:29	15	11:21	16	
1 Kings		21:15, 18	14	12:27-43	47	
2:10	33			12:31-43	16	
2:37	20	2 Chronicles		12:37	15	
3:1	15	1-9	13			
3:3	54	3:1	52	Psalms		
7:1-12	55, 58	4:2-22	53	104	51	
7:15-50	53	7:11	54	137	45	
7:51	60	8:1	54			
8:1	14	8:7	14	Isaiah		
8:12-13	51	8:11	15	22:9	15, 42	
8:23	82	9:16-20	54	22:10	40	

99

22:11	42	31:38-40	18, 20	Ezekiel	
22:16	80	36:9-12	67	9:2	20
32:14	16	36:10	18-19	40-48	55
40:55	59	37:13	18		
		37:21	39	Micah	
Jeremiah		38:7	18	4:8	16
6:1	61	39:3	18-19		
7:17-18	76	39:4	18	Zephaniah	
19	71-2	52:7	18	1:11	39, 64
19:2	18-19, 39	52:17-23	61		
20:2	18, 20			Zechariah	
22:13-19	61	Lamentations		14:10	19
26:10	18-19	1:1	1		
				Acts	
				2:29	2